Douglas Thomp 
national journali
the world's best-
He is a regular
magazines worldwide, including
Express, *Cosmopolitan* and the *New York Daily News*, and has written best-selling biographies of Madonna, Clint Eastwood, Sharon Stone and Michelle Pfeiffer. Based in Los Angeles for over twenty years, he now lives with his wife and daughter in Saffron Waldon, Essex.

Also by Douglas Thompson

LIKE A VIRGIN: Madonna Revealed
CLINT EASTWOOD: Sexual Cowboy
PFEIFFER: Beyond The Age Of Innocence
SHARON STONE: Basic Ambition

Dudley Moore

On the couch

Douglas Thompson

WARNER BOOKS

A *Warner* Book

First published in Great Britain in 1996
by Little, Brown and Company
This edition published by Warner Books in 1997

A CIP catalogue record for this book
is available from the British Library.

ISBN 0 7515 1454 3

Typeset in Berkeley by M Rules
Printed and bound in Great Britain by
Clays Ltd, St Ives plc

Warner Books
A Division of
Little, Brown and Company (UK)
Brettenham House
Lancaster Place
London WC2E 7EN

CONTENTS

For Lesley

ACKNOWLEDGEMENTS

From Dagenham, Essex, to Malibu, California, and a host of places in between, scores of people have helped me attempt to tell the full, often crazy and complex life of Dudley Moore. Most are mentioned in the following book, but for those who felt they were being too indiscreet to be named I offer my thanks. Also my regards to Dudley Moore for the good humour, co-operation and interviews over the years.

Special thanks to Barbara Boote at Little, Brown and, as always, extraordinary thanks to literary agent Judith Chilcote.

Circle of Life

'There was total devotion, total involvement. It's enthusiasm that makes it happen. It makes anything happen, I suppose.'

Dudley Moore on his relationship with
Peter Cook

On a warm Monday morning in May 1995 in North London, Dudley Moore was one of a few hundred people – a large number of them the best-known comic and satirical writing talents in Britain – who attended the memorial service for his one-time partner and long-time friend Peter Cook. It was a Pete 'n' Dud sort of occasion with a *Beyond the Fringe* crowd, and the sun came out for them, flashing through the trees around at John's Parish Church in Hampstead. It had been some months since Cook's death at the beginning of the year and Moore had moved on from shock and grief to the need to celebrate the memory of the man with whom he had found fame.

In church he played their cheerful, chirpy serenade 'Goodbye-ee', which in 1965 won ten weeks in the British pop charts, with Dudley on the piano and Peter Cook doing vocals. Outside, mixing with the many who had come to pay tribute to Cook, including Spike Milligan, John Cleese, Barry Humphries, Alan Bennett, Ben Elton, Harry Enfield, Willy Rushton, Michael Palin and Sir David Frost, Dudley was the centre of attention. The girls from the radio stations were all over him with their microphones and questions. The television cameras zoomed in on his rather pale face and dark glasses, but he was brighter than his maroon shirt – and funny. When one remarkably shaped lady enquired how Cook would be feeling, looking down on the morning's events, Dudley ran his eyes up and down her, and up again before saying: 'Or looking up.'

It's not always Hell being 'Cuddly Dudley'.

Dudley Moore likes the ladies. The bigger and taller, the better. His affection has normally been returned. While other famous faces found shade beneath the churchyard trees and traded stories about the sadly departed Peter Cook (aged 57, from a gastrointestinal haemorrhage after years of vodka breakfasts), Dudley was asked for autographs. He signed his name again and again, a true transatlantic, if somewhat tarnished, star. Some of the other 'faces' at St John's looked tired and worn – they looked their age. Dudley Moore looked the part of the international celebrity. He wore his confidence like a protective suit, and the brown eyes performed the required stellar twinkles and the Beverly Hills teeth provided the perfect smile. He was H-O-L-L-Y-W-O-O-D, not 'Beyond the Fringe'.

'Like wine,' he says, 'I'm better with age.'

Shortly before the memorial service, on 19 April, he had turned 60.

A few weeks after the ceremonies, on 28 June 1995, his fourth wife, redhead Nicole Rothschild, 30, gave birth to their son Nicholas Anthony, who arrived weighing 6lb 9oz.

It was a contented moment for Moore after a crazy courtship. He was accused of trying to throttle Nicole on the evening of the Oscars in 1994 and was arrested and handcuffed by the Los Angeles Police Department (LAPD), becoming Prisoner No: 90792032194. Both he and his wife-to-be had dialled 911 – the American emergency services – following a ferocious dispute at his $3 million home in Venice, out on the Pacific coast west of Los Angeles.

Dudley went into a violent rage when Paul Newman appeared on their television screen and Nicole made a disparaging comment about Newman's looks and age. That remark led to another, and another, and finally to the Ventura police precinct and a charge of 'cohabitational abuse'. Not quite Hugh Grant, who bought sex on Sunset Strip, but the tabloid headlines still screamed 'The Shame of Dudley Moore'.

Like many such domestic matters, when the crunch came Nicole did not want to press charges. She wanted to kiss and make up. Nevertheless, her lover was held for more than two hours before being released on $50,000 bail. And it wasn't 'Goodbye-ee' to Nicole.

The anger and acrimony soon went and they began their wedding day with champagne, before Dudley and Nicole tottered off very merrily to the altar. This involved a 10-minute civil ceremony in Marina Del Rey, which is a wander along the coast from Dudley's custom-built, pink-painted home with its turreted sun-roof and a jacuzzi built for two. After the sunset wedding there was more champagne and red wine, and somersaults on and in the sand, with Dudley giggling much like his constantly inebriated 'Arthur' character. As the guests munched crab cakes and *calamari* he bubbled redundantly: 'We've been drinking a lot of champagne.'

Then it was back to his home, which is packed with antiques and recording equipment. There are also two sleek back-to-back grand pianos (Steinway and Yamaha), as well as a battered brown-stained English Normelle Victorian upright with pull-out brass candlestick-holders and wooden inlay, which cost six pounds when Dudley learned to play at his parents' council house in Dagenham, Essex, during World War Two.

With his mother's piano came a reproduction Sheraton stool with a broken handle, which as a five-year-old Dudley had to push back into place again and again during lessons so that it would not collapse.

No amount of money would tempt him to part with these memories of the past. To him they are priceless. The piano and stool were traced to a store-house in Essex and bought for him, and imported to California at great cost by his third wife, Brogan Lane. She wanted Dudley to be 'at peace' with his 'roots', after listening to some maudlin talk one evening that ended with him saying: 'I wish I could see that piano again.'

He was married to the one-time model christened Denise Brogan while he was seeing Nicole Rothschild, who was then married to musician Charles Cleveland.

It was typical of Dudley to involve himself not in a

love triangle but a lusty quadrangle. He's an involve-ment-at-first-sight man. And, partly because of this, he's dragged much emotional baggage with him throughout his life, troubled, never satisfied and his own worst enemy. The hysterical funny man – the silly voice offered on command – has always been a pre-tence; there are inner doubts and agonies, rather than tears, with this clown.

But in the summer of 1995 he was once again a dot-ing dad. The diminutive Dudley loved his 'little Nikki', as opposed to 'big Nikki' Nicole, and showered atten-tion and gifts on him just as he had indulged his mother. Most of the gifts to Nicole – the cars, jewellery and clothes – were directly for her, but her two breast implants, costing $11,000, were more for Dudley's enjoyment. He has always had a mammary fascination.

Sharing his parenthood joy was Nicole's ex-husband Charles Cleveland. Forget the Bradys. It was the Bizarre Bunch. The new, all-male Dudley Moore Trio.

There was Dud, his newborn son and Cleveland, who had become the man-about-the-house in the comic star's somewhat novel, and certainly intriguing, domestic arrangements in California.

Nicholas Anthony Moore was 9½ inches tall when he was born. His dad is a 5ft 2in-high self-confessed sex thimble. And 35-year-old Cleveland is a strapping six-footer. But the grown-ups said then that statistics didn't count. Love did. There were many oohs and ahhs about life's new arrival and when they posed for the first baby pictures, Californian photographer Phil Ramey found himself snapping Dudley, his new son – and Cleveland.

They were all part of one happy family, which included Nicole (5ft 8in tall), who had enjoyed an off-the-wall, long-time affair and 15-month marriage with Dudley before their son was born.

Success bought Dudley, among other trinkets, a 1963 white Bentley (number plate 'TNDRLY') and provided a champagne lifestyle. Which he was happy to share with his wife, her former husband and, in the summer of 1995, most importantly, with his new son. Dudley, who attended the birth of Nicholas – as did Charles Cleveland – said: 'I couldn't have been more delighted. It was just marvellous. It's 20 years since my son Patrick was born and the years do make you forget what a joy it is. It makes you appreciate everything about life when you see it arriving. I've got no worries about being an older father. Nicole keeps me young – and I've got someone else to live life to the full for. He's a wonderful bundle. I love every minute of fatherhood. I just look at Nicholas and cry tears of joy.'

Cleveland answered the obvious questions: 'I know it may seem strange for Dudley to allow me into the delivery room, but Nicole and I are more like brother and sister than former spouses.'

For Dudley, the baby boy was another chance.

He has had a difficult relationship with his son Patrick – 'Patch' to his friends – from his five-year marriage to American actress and Sixties beauty Tuesday Weld. Following the divorce she moved to New York and Dudley stayed in California. Trans-continent parenting made communications with his son difficult. He still finds it a strain with Patrick, whose photographs dominate his bedroom wall. Dudley understands the horror of alienation.

This time around he was intent on being an on-the-spot father. And he had the support of Nicole – and Charles Cleveland, who was a 14-year-old busker in Germany when he joined up with the John Lee Hooker band, before moving on solo to Motown and American concerts.

Cleveland revealed that Nicole – they have two children, Lauren and Christopher, who were respectively eight and seven in 1995 – had indulged in almost a decade-long affair with Dudley. He said that the highly charged sexual relationship continued while Dudley was married to statuesque, Southern-drawling actress Brogan Lane.

But any hurt over being cuckolded by Dudley has since vanished. And any misgivings Dudley may have had over his wife's ex-husband moving in have also disappeared. Dudley has been on a matrimonial merry-go-round all his life but, like the title of one of his old films, he's been *bedazzled* by Nicole, whom he calls 'Honeybunny' in their many amorous moments.

But it wasn't always non-stop loving, although Dudley is credited with being a five-times-a-day sexual pixie – even when he has a headache.

He knows he's difficult to live with and has bought his wife a $600,000 home just 500 yards from his own lavish waterfront accommodation.

He had a similar arrangement with Brogan Lane. During that marriage they both maintained separate homes on either side of Los Angeles. He was in Venice and she had a wonderful, clapboard, chocolate-box house in Toluca Lake.

With Nicole he even hired Charles Cleveland at $75 a day to play 'nanny' to his own children. They would all spend the evening together and often Dudley would then return to his own home. 'That way if we needed some space we just had to go a few blocks to get it,' he explained, without any hint that this might be an extra-ordinary set-up.

But with the birth of Nicholas, the Moore ensemble moved down the Californian coast to the exotically expensive coastal resort of Newport Beach, where boat berths sell for more than $1 million. They were all to be living in *one* house in the town Moore called 'serene and suburban', but which is in reality the Californian capital of money-knows-best, with palm-lined streets laden with Rolls-Royces, Mercedes, Porsches and avarice. And Dudley's right-hand-drive imported Bentley.

Newport Beach is where Nicole Rothschild grew up, and Dudley was more than willing to indulge the mother of his beloved baby boy.

It made a change. During most of his life and many loves Dudley has usually indulged himself. He had, and retains, a chip on both shoulders, has spent years in psychotherapy ('I've been having a mid-life crisis since I was two weeks old – I went right from a midwife to the mid-life crisis') and what seems, to friends, like years on the telephone recounting his anguish and agonies.

He has married four times: Suzy Kendall (1968–72); Tuesday Weld (1975–80); Brogan Lane (1988–90); Nicole Rothschild (1994 to who-knows-when . . .). But, even at 60, Dudley admits he is still afraid of women. 'Oh, yeah, blimey – I've got no idea what makes them tick. Nothing. I have no idea. I don't understand them.'

During and between romantic tangles – and on one occasion while performing off-stage when he should have been performing on-stage – he has displayed his skills as a multi-talented musician, writer, comedy star and actor. And, much to his and many other people's surprise, was a Hollywood heart-throb at the age of 44. Then an American magazine voted him as the man most women wanted to sleep with. They couldn't have picked a more willing candidate.

That particular incident in his life began with legendary director Blake Edwards, who, as well as Peter Sellers' *Pink Panther* series, was responsible for landmark films such as *Breakfast at Tiffany's*, *Days of Wine and Roses*, *S.O.B.* and *The Great Race*.

Their collaboration began on a couch – but not the casting couch. The two first met while attending a psychoanalysis group in Los Angeles. Sounds crazy? It was.

CHAPTER 1

Sex Symbol

'The ability to enjoy your sex life is central. I don't give a shit about anything else. My obsession is total. What else is there to live for?'

one-time choirboy Dudley Moore

Julie Andrews – the two words, not the lady herself – were the magic utterings that brought all the fantasies to reality for short-order cook Dudley, who sells his soul to the Devil in the 1968 movie *Bedazzled*. A little more than a decade later he was co-starring with Andrews, aka Mrs Blake Edwards, in *10*, a film that set all sorts of standards, established Dudley's star credentials and created an international sensation out of Bo Derek.

Dudley rather stumbled and stuttered into movie history. 'After two or three weeks in group therapy with Blake Edwards, he asked me if I would be interested in doing a series of films called *The Ferret*, which was a spin-off of Peter Sellers' Inspector Clouseau, and we came to an agreement about that. He really didn't get to know me except from chatting in group sessions, which was about life, death and all those things. Wonderful subjects! For three weeks I dominated the situation. I just sort of threw my garbage on the floor and said: "What the hell do I do with it?" And I think Blake, not fascinated exactly, was taken by my bleatings. I think he knew of the work that I'd done. He felt I had an ingenious quality, which I suppose from time to time when I'm not tired I do have. I admired his expertise with comedy.

'He was very relaxed. He's not a man who is easy to get to know immediately: he's quite self-contained in many ways. I know he wanted *10* to work commercially, but while we were doing it I didn't get any feeling of the enormous stakes involved.'

Edwards, a complex man with a penchant for darkened glasses, had turned his back on Hollywood following what he regarded as the 'butchered' editing by MGM Studios of his 1972 film *The Carey Treatment*, which starred the lean and tall James Coburn. He went off to Europe to film the *Pink Panther* movies. The films with Peter Sellers' Inspector Clouseau were such enormous hits that Edwards was tempted back to Hollywood with a three-picture deal for the now-defunct Orion Pictures. It was sun, surf's up, Malibu and group therapy.

'He was in one group and I was in another,' recalls Dudley, adding: 'Then, the groups were merged, we joined forces. It just seemed to be someone was dealing the cards my way. It can pay off to be neurotic. We were with a man called Dr Wexler and it was a very good time. Blake was doing *10* with George Segal, but Segal walked and Blake thought: "Who am I going to get?" And he thought of me.'

At the time George Segal was at the top of his fame. He had found much success with *10*-style movies like *A*

Touch of Class with Glenda Jackson in 1973 and the hilarious *Blume in Love* the same year. With hindsight, he would probably have wanted to do things differently, but he felt he was in a strong bargaining position. He objected to script changes on *10*, which he believed favoured Edwards' wife Julie Andrews. Edwards stood by his new script – and as filming was about to begin, lost his leading man.

The sun shone on Dudley, who recalled: 'It was certainly a great opportunity to have met Blake Edwards when I did, but I was primed to go and one way or another I would have forced myself into a situation and gotten some movie going.' But probably not such a landmark event.

Dudley Moore was predestined, it seems, to step in as George Webber, a 42-year-old four-time Oscar-winning musician with all the money and secular comforts he needs, including a high-tech voyeur's telescope, a Rolls-Royce and his girlfriend 'Sam', played by Julie Andrews. This is late Seventies early Eighties Los Angeles and specifically the world surrounding Pacific Coast Highway and Beverly Hills. George Webber and others in this playpen don't want for anything. 'Sam' accuses George of 'ogling' young bosoms and bottoms down his telescope.

But Dudley/George wants more. He rates the passing parade of femininity on a scale from 1 to 10. He's a tough judge, giving the Venus de Milo a soft 7 – and that's if she had arms; 10, you can almost hear him sing, is the impossible dream. Not for Blake Edwards.

George seems to have forgotten or mislaid a couple of years of his existence. He's in the grip of mid-life panic. Youth is surfing before him – in his mind, and on the beach at the end of the lens of that titillating telescope. And then George Webber has an erotic epiphany as he motors through Beverly Hills. In the next car he sees Bo Derek as a ravishing bride – a 20 on his scale of 1 to 10 beauty – and he becomes a madcap, romantic Don Quixote. He starts tilting at her tenderloins. In his mind.

In the film, which is a blend of farce and Blake Edwards' mix of bitter-sweet and slapstick comedy, Webber, who sees so much outside that he is blinkered about himself, becomes libidinally obsessed with his quest for the 'Perfect Woman', who is Bo Derek in super shape and with corn-plait hairstyle. His quest takes him to the $55 million tourist paradise of Las Hadas ('The Fairies') on Mexico's bougainvillaea coast and, finally, into her bed – but then the dream flakes like a careless suntan.

The location – a haunt for pirates, a kingdom of minarets and domes, towers and turrets, blending Moorish, Mediterranean and Mexican motifs – was the perfect spot for Webber's obsession. It was a playpen for porpoises and a rainbow of tropical fish, and he would find out that he was just another drop in that phosphorus-fuelled ocean. Not so much a fish but a wanna-be-philanderer out of water.

Dudley had been writing a similar but – understandably for him – greedier story about a man chasing *several* fantasy women. After the psychological sauna with Edwards and other West-Coast seekers of mental clarity he decided to 'become' George Webber and 'filed' his screenplay: 'I didn't want to get involved in trying to change the script of *10* at that stage.

'I told Blake I wanted to play it straight and he agreed. Most of my film parts until then had been over-laid with caricature. And I had a few minutes with him about the shittiness of the character, of his bad temper. But Blake wanted him to be edgy and brittle and I accepted that.

'In my story the man wasn't so much afraid of grow-ing old but keen to live his life and meet all the fantastic girls and people he wanted – but there was a certain urgency about it, because he was getting on.

'The film sort of combines the fear of growing old and the idea of someone fantasising about this girl he believes is going to charm him for ever, and he thinks he is going to be very special for her.'

Dudley has spent a lifetime, since losing his virginity ('properly') aged 23, searching for his perfect woman, *his* '10' – the love of his life, someone who will under-stand him and whom he, in turn, will be able to deal with. He always wants to be the focus of attention, and clearly in any relationship that is not always possible.

He's thought about it: 'Floating from woman to woman is fine by me. People get rather moral about it. They feel that the responsibility for sex and what hap-pens next lies in the man's hands. Actually it's 50-50. I make sure that it's a mutual decision.

'Women often accuse men who have made love to them of "using" them. Surely, when a man makes love to a woman neither owes the other anything. You have to say: "I can't promise you anything." And you can't. Not before the encounter, anyway. Afterwards, who knows?

'Still, passion is a great holder of two people together. If a woman or man is passionate enough to know how to take pleasure, then they give it by enjoying themselves. Then you stick around more.'

10 introduced Bo Derek to the world and, aged 22, she became a phenomenon. It was her second film – she was the girl who struggled with the shark in *Orca* in 1977 – and she was paid $35,000 for showing off her stunning body to Dudley and, thankfully for all concerned, millions and millions of movie-goers around the world. 'She was young and beautiful but she wasn't a bimbo type,' recalls Dudley, adding: 'This was a girl who had a head on her beautiful body. None of us could ever have imagined what a fantastic reaction there would be to her. She was George Webber's fantasy, and as far as I and Blake Edwards were concerned that was the script. Then, of course, the whole world wanted Bo – she was *the* 10.'

Finding his '10' was Blake Edwards' greatest challenge. Beauty and sex appeal are obviously subjective. One person's 10 is another's 5½. Hollywood being like a hyperactive telephone exchange, the message flashed around the casting grapevine that co-ordinates model agencies, small theatres, actors, agents, aspiring actresses, the wine bars and coffee shops.

We want a GREAT body, was the message.

On one casting-call afternoon twelve of the most sought-after commercial models in the world – the Claudia Schiffers, Cindy Crawfords and Christy Turlingtons of their day – wearing underwear they chose themselves were screen-tested in sequence. The casting people had, like George Webber, their 1 to 10 scorecards. But looks were not enough. They wanted acting talent as well. Then, Bo Derek arrived. Edwards is still amazed how casual and modest she was: 'Her first words when she came in to read for us were: "I'm sorry about wasting your time." Meanwhile, Tony Adams, who co-produced the movie with me, and I were crossing our fingers and hoping: "Let her be able to act, please let her be able to act." She could. She was a delight. And with Dudley there was great rapport. They were both pretty new to Hollywood, so they could understand each other's doubts and concerns. They were like another couple of kids for Julie and I to look after. Dudley was adorable and open and fun.'

And the newspaper and billboard advertisements made the most of bountiful Bo. They zeroed in on her breasts and navel. Her co-star Julie Andrews, despite desperately trying to lose her 'Mary Poppins' image, was not happy with the marketing campaign: 'I happen to be a very liberated lady and I considered the campaign to be in very bad taste – and extremely foolish.' The British-born star was also anxious about criticism of her four-lettered language in *10* which in our late-Nineties Quentin Tarantino movie days seems quaintly acceptable. She was quick to respond: 'I'm damned if I do and damned if I don't. I would like to be considered an actress rather than "Mary Poppins" for the rest of my life.'

Julie Andrews' quest to change her squeaky-clean image continued as she starred in her husband's hilarious and clever satire of Hollywood, *S.O.B.*, in which she bared her breasts, and as the lady who pretends to be a man who pretends to be a lady in *Victor/Victoria*.

Nevertheless, she played 'Mary Poppins' to Dudley. She was a 'nanny' in the sense that she tutored him, as a fellow-Briton, on the perils of Hollywood and of 'overnight' success. He leaned on her and on his couch-partner Blake Edwards.

Bo Derek was getting similar lessons from her husband John Derek, the Forties matinée idol who was later more famous for his ex-wives – Princess Patti Behrs, Ursula Andress and Linda Evans – and their bizarre friendships with each other and with Bo. He was determined that his young bride would not be exploited in the way he felt he had been by 'the Hollywood machine'.

Dudley was receiving multi-million-dollar offers and so was Bo. Dudley went for it. Bo Derek decided to work with her husband. Getting on for 20 years later the question is: Who did get it right? The answer is up to the beholder. Dudley admits that he is still not sure, but it's clear he does envy Bo's lifestyle.

You see the Dereks' house first from Monte Cielo – 'the mountain to heaven' – and it sits so high up in the hills that the Mexican-tiled roof appears to be touching the clear California sky. This is horse country, and you get here by driving for 45 minutes on sweeping, curving roads to the north of Santa Barbara. Then it's bouncing dirt tracks until you spot the arrow with a red heart tacked to a telephone pole, pointing the way to the electronic security gates.

That's the only Tinseltown touch in the lifestyle of Bo and John Derek. They're Hollywood's back-to-basics couple.

And it was a life that kept Bo in good enough shape to adorn the pages of *Playboy* magazine again – 15 years after her début she was the main cover in December 1994. Inside, she was the stapled centrefold attraction in photographs taken by her husband.

The Dereks live lavishly but not at all in the way perception tells us glamour queens do. Or maybe should. Their Spanish hacienda is stunning and so is Bo Derek, who bounces around bra-less in a white sweatshirt and faded working ranch jeans. She knows the other sort of genes were generous to her and says she still feels guilty about it. She was 40 in 1996 but for Hollywood and, clearly, *Playboy* remains a '10'.

After that huge hit she more or less bowed out of mainstream Hollywood. Until the mid-Nineties her life was her home and her husband. Times change. Necessity brought her back to the spotlight.

It was the comparatively modest money earned from that box-office success that helped make the down-payment on their lovingly nourished 26 acres in the

Santa Ynez Valley. The movie that made Dudley a Hollywood star and self-confessed 'sex thimble' – a reputation he has proved again and again – also established Bo Derek. She has fond memories of Dudley and says: 'Nothing would surprise me about him. He's cheeky and likes to have fun. Which is fine if no one gets hurt. I just hope Dudley and his ladies are okay.

'It was all new to me and for Dudley, despite all his successes, it was something tremendous. That fame when it hits – especially in America – is very hard to deal with. He did. He laughed along with it. There's not many people who could have coped so well. And he enjoyed it. That was the wonderful part. He didn't suddenly take himself all serious. He prepared, he worked hard in the movie and it took off and so did he. That's special.'

John and Bo Derek were at that time living in an apartment in Marina Del Rey, where Dudley would later marry, when Bo became a worldwide fantasy girl and not just the fascination of cinema audiences but of every producer with minimal eyesight.

'John really saw the necessity to get out right away and have a place. We didn't have the money but with the few dollars we had, we made a down-payment and thought we'd worry about it later. It's been my sanity, this life.

'And it's not just the ranch and the animals (27 horses, cats, dogs and parrots in 1995), but being with real people who have nothing to do with the film business. We're involved with the community – if someone is in trouble or has problems everybody tries to help. We're more social than I ever believed we'd be.

'Now there's a big invasion of film people up here. I don't like it, because they don't leave their business down in Hollywood. We'll be sitting around having lunch with friends and someone who's in the business will come in and they can't talk about anything except how much money they just turned down, how much they're worth, how much the picture made and, oh, it's so boring . . .'

What is not boring, she says happily, is her life with John, who turned a beach-loving blonde Californian teenager called Mary Cathleen Collins into a star. He called her 'Bo' and helped create a sensation.

Derek was still married to Linda 'Dynasty' Evans when he met her lookalike on a Greek island. Although he was 30 years older, they were smitten by each other. And still are. 'I'm just about the luckiest person in the world. I've only known love. I went right from my family who love me to John. I found my love when I was 17 years old and my love is 100 per cent honest. We've never had any ugly, rocky things to overcome.

'This love and this lifestyle are everything I hold as the ultimate thing to have in life. This is something to envy and I'm so happy to have it. Others would rather have jewellery and cars and furs or whatever is opulent. But this is opulence to me, and I'm ashamed to have it sometimes. I work hard, for I feel I have to earn it somehow, to do more than just have a straight nose.'

The Dereks designed their own gardens and stables,

and over the years have added outbuildings and horse-working areas. Every plant, every brick on the property has been personally approved. John Derek would put in trees before lunch and then take them out afterwards and vice-versa. He is a fickle perfectionist. He has always wanted everything around him to be beautiful. By the front door is a navy-blue lap-pool installed to help Mrs Derek keep her assets firm. She also takes pills to stop water-retention. Even '10's need help for a fabulous figure.

It's a figure she's displayed in films like *Tarzan, The Ape Man* and *Bolero*, but she denies she's made 'sexy' films and announces: 'I feel like such a prude now. I never thought I would feel prudish in this business and about film projects. You haven't even begun to see the films that are coming. I've been reading screenplays . . . these vulgar women, these wild sex scenes and I mean they just . . . if they don't get more inventive there's nothing else you can do.

'It's been done to death and it's vulgar just to be vulgar. I find them so unappealing and so unattractive. The next group of films is just unbelievable. Sharon Stone? It all boils down to who she's making love to and why she's making love in the story. The gymnastics pretty much haven't changed. I think Madonna is the only one who goes over the edge on that.

'I played a definite part in it. I guess the things that I played in films, and the way the nudity and the love scenes were handled, were really different. What now stands out as unusual is that in the love scenes I did the people were in love. It wasn't kinky, deviant – any of these things that seem to be most popular right now in the 1990s. There's an incredible fascination for that, and that goes with violence and everything else in pictures.'

She does not have concerns for actresses getting involved in torrid scenes: 'I don't feel sorry for them at all. What's there to feel sorry about? They're simulating sex in a film. I find it much worse to simulate sick violence and glamorise it – that's something to worry about, and that I would have trouble with my conscience doing. Glorifying violence is terrible. Simulating sex is nothing – it's something so impersonal really.'

She keeps reading scripts, and in 1995 was gently putting herself back in the Hollywood workplace. She drives down to town during the week for meetings and stays with friends. And she can still laugh at the days when the world's producers were constantly knocking at her door: 'We had people walking into the office with suitcases full of money and taking millions and millions, and big percentages of billions of dollars, and it was so overwhelming. When I look back on it, it was so much fun to turn down, more fun than accepting it. I get a kick out of it and I smile when I think about it. In the long run I've had much more fun having turned them down.

'A lot of people think I've missed out, but I don't think I have. It's always been my decision. I've got experience now to defend myself against a monster director – I couldn't before, I didn't know the game.

'We moved here because we couldn't stand the bullshit that goes with being a so-called celebrity and living in a glass house. We love making movies but we don't like all the hangers-on, all the pretence that goes into this business. I have a reputation for being difficult, as well as for being under John's influence. They think I am just a body for him to channel through.'

She and John have for the most part been a working-couple package. By 1995, however, she travelled and did deals on her own. 'I never felt dependent on him but at the same time I think I knew deep inside that this was all too much for me to handle alone. It's a certain type of dependency but it's also a partnership and sharing. Looking back on myself, I could never have handled all the attention *10* brought.

'I met John in 1974. It's amazing, isn't it? I've changed so much. I thought at the time I was very adult and mature and grown-up, but now when I look back at myself, at 16, 17, 18, 19, 20 – up to about 32 – I was very young, very, very, very young. But you never realise that at the time. I wasn't a woman.'

She is now. And part of the *Playboy* deal and its publicity was aimed at keeping the family's future intact. She also appeared in the chilly thriller *Billy The Third*.

John Derek, 69 in 1995, had a heart attack eight years earlier and suffered a slight stroke in 1991. It made him even more aware of his own mortality and the 30-year age difference in his marriage. He thinks often of 15 years down the line and says: 'It will be awful for her, because I will be slowly falling apart and no matter what she says the person she fell in love with won't be there any more.'

He knows his wife. She dismisses his concerns with 'I'm not going to worry about anything until it happens. It's not my nature. I very much live for the moment and if it's a good day, it's a good day.

'And if tomorrow is supposed to be a bad day, I'll wait until tomorrow and deal with it when it comes. Which just seems logical to me, because you can't predict how you are going to react to something. That's what I'm told, so why should I try? He always said I'd leave but I don't, I don't.

'John goes through dark periods. His blood pressure is through the roof but thanks to the advances of modern medicine . . . he takes about sixty pills a day. No, I'm exaggerating. But a lot of pills, all different colours. It's all under control and he leads a fairly normal life. He's going through a bright, happy stage right now, but he does get moody.

'He's very unsatisfied with the world in general, not just in our lives. He can watch the news and just go into a funk for a long time.

'He doesn't worry about the future – he jokes about it. He doesn't very often have serious conversations about it. We're both intelligent enough people to know that certain things are going to happen eventually, but it's still a long way off.

'As I mature – we've been together 20 years – the age gap and the personality gap and all these things just start to get smaller and smaller and you become more similar.

'Rarely does he ever get me confused with his other blonde wives now . . . He used to say: "Remember when we went here or there, and did this?" I'd say: "No, that wasn't me." We'd argue and he'd say: "Oh, that was the other blonde."' Bo has said in the past that she was waiting until the right time to have children, but now she admits: 'I don't want children now. John has always been open to having children if I wanted, but they're not his favourite things. He doesn't care for them that much. I don't want them any more. I never seriously did. It's something you're supposed to want as a woman and I've been saying: "Oh, maybe in a few years." I don't even say that any more. John prefers animals and, yeah, I prefer animals. The more I learn about people and animals, people aren't very nice.'

Nevertheless, they are surrounded by people as well as animals. Famous people.

Michael Jackson's Neverland ranch is a short drive away. 'Elizabeth's wedding was there. We have Steven Seagal and Kelly Le Brock now. We have Jimmy Connors and his Patti, who's a very good friend of mine. They've been here a long time, though. We have John Forsythe – he just moved up and bought a really cute goat farm here. We have Cheryl Ladd and her husband Brian. There's Fess Parker and Ray Stark, the producer, and the producer Doug Cramer.

'The Reagans? Yes, Ronald and Nancy – they don't come very often now. It's so sad about his illness. It's a very remote place they have, and it's a nice old house but it's not luxurious.'

They are also surrounded by rumours. There was one that she and Ursula Andress and Linda Evans – John Derek's trio of wives remain close friends – were going to open a restaurant together. 'I used to take the rumours seriously and now I just exaggerate. When they call and ask about the restaurant I say: "Yes, we're opening on Rodeo Drive in Beverly Hills and then having 26 more across the country. Sort of Italian Hard Rock Cafés."

'The last rumour was that we were so broke we were selling our ranch for $20 million. I loved that. I'd love to have assets of $20 million.

'Dudley must have millions. He was 20 years older than me when he got his chance. And it was a big chance. He took it. He really went for it and I think it was clearly the right thing to do.'

Blake Edwards still shakes his head at his luck in getting Dudley for *10*. 'As you know, it was only by chance that it happened. Throughout my career I have learned to take the moment or play the hunch, or whatever you want to call it, but we all know this was perfect casting. *Angst* and insecurity and a passion and yearning to fulfil. Dudley was perfect.'

Circumstances were not always so favourable. The opening scene of *10* is a drunken birthday at Malibu beach house. The night before the main filming began a brush fire swept through the Santa Monica Mountains, and down and across Pacific Coast Highway in Malibu. More than 200 homes were destroyed and hundreds of people evacuated. Then the rains arrived and the film's co-producer Tony Adams moved out his family before his home was hit by a mud-slide. Blake Edwards and Julie Andrews kept an all-night vigil over their beach home.

It was rain off a duck's back for Dudley. He just wanted to get on with filming. And they did. The following day, with the fire contained, Edwards wandered around the beach house that was to be the first *10* location.

The fire had come to within 10 feet. The beach house was slightly singed. Filming began. It was a difficult real and fantasy world, as Dudley remembers: 'Blake did superficially give us lots of things to deal with: drunkenness, falling down hills. He made an accumulation of accidents and small tragedies, and I suppose George in *10* is in some torment about it but finds some sort of answer. That there is no answer.

'Blake and I seemed to get on very well. In a couple of areas I would disagree with him in terms of stress in the film. For example, the argument about the term "broad". I felt as an Englishman that I wouldn't have used it. And I wasn't sure I wanted to play the character so grumpy, but I agreed with him in the end that it was probably useful for him to be in that irritable mood. There wasn't anything that went against the grain.

'I was worried about singing the song in the end with Julie Andrews. I felt it was a razor's edge of sentimentality, but I did it and I felt happy with it afterwards. I'd never done anything like that before. I don't sing. I mean, I *do* sing, I've sung all my life. But it was weird to sing a sentimental, romantic tune with Julie Andrews and I expressed a lot of apprehension about it. But it worked and the edge was taken of it, for it slipped in humour.

'I found the nude scene quite difficult – it was an interesting experiment – but I didn't argue with Blake about that. I agreed it would be funny and it was necessary to see that I was nude, so that when Julie looks at me through the telescope it would be obvious.

'It was good with Blake. He doesn't direct. He just sort of lets you do it. We didn't really discuss it very much, except the bedroom scene with Bo Derek when we're talking in the end. We did that a few times, which was unusual, because most of the time it was one or two takes. He was very concerned about having variations in the end too. He's very relaxed when he works. He works very quietly, setting the shots. When he's looking for what he wants there's total silence, but then there's a very easy atmosphere when he's shooting.

'We had a lot of laughs. As I said, he doesn't really direct, which is a great talent for a director to have – not to interfere.'

Dudley Moore was 44, going on 45, when *10* was made and presented worldwide, and he said: 'The most valuable thing on screen is someone showing himself.'

And he was perfect for George Webber. A man with absolutely everything. And nothing. 'The role wasn't rewritten for me. It was extraordinary that I was all the things that this man was in the film. The only thing we dropped was smoking a cigar, which I don't do. I didn't want to wear sun-glasses but Blake kept insisting. I think he wanted me to wear them because he wears them all the time. I did some preparation for George Webber but I didn't go into any sort of great trance. I enjoyed doing it and it was easy, relaxing work. I prepare for my roles depending on the intricacies of the character, but you only have to think of it while you are doing it on-camera. I never want to overlay the character with too much extra stuff. I only filled in the thoughts – what the man was thinking, feeling, wanting.'

That would be sex?

'Details of his behaviour I didn't think about too much. They come naturally out of me. Everything seemed to develop out of the situation in time and in his head. It all imploded.'

Of course, his career exploded. In *10* he appears stark-naked in an orgy scene with lots of magnificently bosomed nude girls. He has a bed scene with Bo Derek, who enquires unromantically (more like a blow-up doll than a flesh fantasy): 'Would you like to fuck?'

He says, straight-faced, that he got in shape for the sequence on a diet of Brussels sprouts for breakfast and nothing else all day. As with most things in his life, he made a joke out of his demons but admitted: 'I felt quite traumatised, especially when the lighting cameraman fell on the floor laughing. There I am, all over the screen. Well, you couldn't see any particles. It was the first time my mum had seen me like that for years.'

His mother was his link to reality. She died in 1981. Her son is now in his sixties. And he's frank about it: '30 was more of a crisis for me than 40; 40 slipped by and 50 went by – just like that! And with 60 I had no trouble at all.

'The dilemma that George Webber found himself caught up with in *10* is something that I've struggled with in one way or another for ever. Really, all I ever wanted was love. I basically played myself in *10*. It was the first movie I was comfortable enough to finally play myself, which is why I think it worked so well.

'Not only in terms of personal relationships but in dealing with life in general. The way Julie Andrews is tall and was cast as my girlfriend in *10* was good. Height really doesn't matter where sex is concerned. (When I was involved with Susan Anton who *is* tall I used to say I went *up* on her). There's a marvellous English ice about Julie and you don't have to chip very hard to get at the fire. She's delicious. Julie's not the sugar-sweet person everybody believes her to be, thank goodness. She's a very sexy actress. She can deal with life. I am always having to understand the reality of things and people.'

For 'people' one should really read women. There have been so many of them. Some he will rate on the '10' scale – others he prefers to say little about. His first wife Suzy Kendall gets full marks: 'Ten out of ten physically, emotionally and spiritually. She's one of those rare girls who look good any time, day or night. Why divorce her? I couldn't stand the competition.'

35

After their break-up he dated tiny singer Lynsey de Paul for three months, but the I-love-them-tall-and-well-built syndrome ended the relationship. 'I don't think I want to say anything about him,' was Ms de Paul's reaction.

But Dudley talked about Julie Christie: 'Another ten. We went out for a time and neither of us had any complaints. Fascinating, fantastic lady.'

And Jane Fonda: 'I'd give her an eight. Physically she's perfect but she can be a bit too serious. I'm all for chatting to birds, but there are certain moments when actual action takes precedence.'

And Faye Dunaway: 'Nine. A dream. Everything you fantasise about her is true, and more! She loses a point simply because she called it a day with me. Out of etiquette our parting should have been a mutual decision.'

And Vanessa Redgrave: 'A five, if you know what I mean. Vanessa could learn a thing or two from Jane Fonda. Old Dud's not very political and I never even knew about suffragettes until I went out with Vanessa. So I wasn't too bright a conversationalist for her.'

And Raquel Welch: 'Off the scale. How can you put a number on the eighth wonder of the world? Mind you, she can be a bit frightening. We used to get all these giant men clustering around us. Several times I nearly got crushed to death in the stampede.'

And Susan George: 'Eight. I used to call her "Sparrow". Quite a bird. Unfortunately she was always trying to get me to take her dogs on long walks. I like to reserve my energy for more unhealthy pursuits.'

And Gina Lollobrigida: 'Seven. Physically great, but I couldn't get used to that Italian temperament. When that flared up I wilted. I'm not that good at eating spaghetti either. There I was, trying to get in my fork, when I should have been . . .'

And Bo Derek is, of course, a '10'.

Most still adore Dudley but there are those, like Lynsey de Paul and stage actress Helen Gill, who do not appear to remember fondly their trysts with the man called by another former girlfriend 'a lecherous pygmy'.

There is a harsh reality to the apparently all-fun-and-games lifestyle of Dudley Moore. There *is* rejection.

It was something Dudley unwittingly faced from the beginning. Moments after he was born he was presented to his mother – a white-wrapped but flawed baby bundle – and she responded to this usually glorious delivery moment with: 'He's not mine. I don't want him. Take him away.'

It was the start of a tortured, talented and tempestuous life, which six decades later he has yet to come completely to terms with. He's still uncomfortable with his life's mix of music, molls, maisonettes and Malibu.

The lad from London's working-class East End, who soared to the scholastic heights of Oxbridge and the sunshine stardom of Hollywood, changed the odds, for he was crippled from the start . . .

CHAPTER TWO

Sex Thimble

'Chinese food and women – there is nothing else.'

Dudley Moore

Dudley is the first to admit that he was an unlikely Hollywood idol. By the time *10* arrived he was much more confident – despite the regular analysis – and could indulge in a lifestyle far, far removed from his Dagenham days. His growing up had been difficult and sometimes cruel. He was born with his feet turned inwards. His right foot corrected itself and surgeons took on the job of the left foot. Despite their valiant efforts over seven years, which involved him in long hospital stays, Dudley was to retain a club foot. His left leg was shorter than his right and withered from the knee down. In the school playground they called him 'Hopalong'.

It is telling that many years later, when he was doing promotional photographs for *10*, he appeared in a picture with a group of incredibly well-endowed nude ladies. He was naked too, apart from a white towel draped around his head and lap – and his left leg.

He had a club foot. He was short. He was, as his friend and *Beyond the Fringe* partner Jonathan Miller called him, 'a grubby cherub'. But he was also, in the description he enjoys most, a sex thimble.

Women wanted to 'care' for Dudley. And he was never about to upset them by saying no. Following his divorce from his second wife Tuesday Weld he met the statuesque actress and singer Susan Anton. She was recovering from a broken love affair with Sylvester Stallone. Her story of their first night together is a capsule of Dudley's romantic success.

'The first time I saw Dudley – at the National Association of Theatre Owners' convention in Las Vegas – he made me laugh, so I went up and introduced myself.

'Later he came to Vegas, where I was performing, to see me. When he came backstage after my show we both thought we'd made a terrible mistake. I'd forgotten how short he was and he'd forgotten how tall I was. After a midnight dinner, I impulsively said, 'Why don't we go to my room? I've got a bottle of wine and we can talk.' So we went there and started talking. And pretty soon I said: 'Do you know what I want to do? I want to go to your room and I want to go to bed with you and I want you to hold me. I'm not ready for anyone to make love to me yet. I just want to be held.' Dudley said okay, and that was our first night together. He just held me and let me cry about everything that hurt me. The next morning, we watched *Wuthering Heights* and we both cried. He cried about his divorce and I cried about my break-up with Sly. And that's how we fell in love.'

From Dagenham to Las Vegas and Susan Anton, who

had won international acclaim in the movie *Goldengirl* about a manufactured athlete.

Dudley had grown up in a manufacturing town. He was born on 19 April 1935, in London's Charing Cross Hospital, and his mother Ada Frances (née Hughes) was aghast when she saw him, but took him home to 14 Monmouth Road. She and her husband John Moore, who worked for nearly four decades as an electrician for British Rail, had been the first tenants of the house built in 1928. It lay a short walk from the Dagenham Tube station, built to accommodate the Ford car plant that had opened in October 1931. Dudley's mother had given up her job as a typist/secretary to look after his sister Barbara, who was born in 1929. For her Dudley – 'named after some Bishop,' he says – was to be a heartache. The Cripple.

He may have looked the part, but Dudley was no Tiny Tim. He landed up in bed with Raquel Welch in *Bedazzled* and with Bo Derek in *10*. He has had count-less love affairs – some that even he can't remember. On the psychiatrist's couch they would probably say he was over-compensating for his deformity and lack of height.

Dudley says he just enjoys sex. It is his life's motiva-tion. And he talks frankly about it. There is no embarrassment. How was on-screen sex for him? 'Well, Raquel played a tempting creature known as Lillian Lust. Holy shit, she really has a great body. When she was supposed to seduce me in the bed scene, I wore three pairs of underpants, thinking, Christ, if I get an erection, maybe three pairs will help. I was thinking of tying my cock down with Band-Aids or something – literally! I thought it was going to be very embarrassing. But that kind of scene ultimately turns out to be unerotic, because you're thinking of something else.

'In *10* and *Bedazzled* I had to do both scenes with both women twice. Hmmmmm, I think a little pattern is emerging here. We were both naked, but they lit it so you couldn't see a damned thing. I was nervous, but Bo wasn't. She had to get up from the bed and walk over to the hi-fi and then go back to the bed. Let me tell you, it wasn't easy for me.

'It is embarrassing to have everyone staring, saying: 'What's she got? What's he got?' You feel more stupid than turned on. You're thinking about your lines, your timing, your camera angle – not about sex.

'Bo is basically cool. I didn't think of her as a sexy person. I don't mean that as an insult. I just mean she doesn't farm it out in public. She's not like Bardot, who used to flirt with the world; nor is there a sensuality, as you have with Anna Karenina or Sophia Loren.

'I think sex is the most important part of anybody's life. *The* most important part. The ability to enjoy your sex life is central. I don't give a shit about anything else. One's desire for another person is the most flattering thing you can take from that person. The best sex you can give anybody is what you take from them with the utmost enthusiasm.

'Women are more important than work. They are the obsession of my life. What else is there to live for?

Chinese food and women – there *is* nothing else. Actually, I sometimes hate women for having such an effect on me.

'I just want to do everything to them. I want to murder them and love them, and embrace them and die in them, and live in them and *all* that stuff. *Everything!* Just go through the dictionary, and that's what I want to do: I want to aardvark them, Afghanistan them, blender them, demarcate them, Zulu them. I want to do *everything*!

'I went to bed with two women. It was fuckin' great. I also tried it once with a male friend and a woman, but we just ended up laughing. I mean, it was like choosing ends: "Which end do you want?" It was so exhilarating we couldn't do anything.

'When I was about 11 I realised I was going to be a prisoner of sex. I looked at girls, and suddenly, all I wanted to do was to love them, have them kiss me. I even remember their names. Joan Harold and Shirley Powell, and Louise McDonald and Jean Dabbs and – oh, fuck . . . Yeah, sex really had me by the ears. I masturbated from five or six on, but it wasn't until a couple of years later that I focused on doing something more with girls.

'As a teenager, I found the idea of intercourse completely frightening. I do remember the first breast I ever fondled. The girl wasn't exactly attractive, but she did have a fair pair of knockers. Anyway, we went behind her house, where I stood on some bricks so I could reach her. Then, as if by remote control, she guided my hand to her breast. I remember feeling this thing and thinking: Oh! – as though I'd put my hand on a sheep's eye, or something.

'Afterwards I felt totally disgraced. I thought: That's it. I've done it now. I've blotted my copybook. That went on for some time – girls and very passionate snogging and smooching, a bit of breast-fondling. But nothing very much of a south-of-waist nature. I remember once at a party sitting frozen in a chair with a girl on my lap. We were both pretending to be asleep, but I felt the sexual electricity just whipping through us. I didn't actually get into any heavy petting until I was about 16 or so and met a French girl. She terrified me. But I still used to visit her in Paris. She had a little garden house, where we'd go and I would venture to insert part of my disgusting body into her, only to withdraw as if we were magnets with opposite poles meeting.

'And, then, of course, I used to wank myself to death over my father's magazines. He had quite a collection. Come to think of it, he's probably also the reason I've fantasised about women with big tits. I mean, show me a fire hydrant and I'll come on the spot. But I also like a nice arse and legs. In the end, of course, none of it makes a damned bit of difference, because it's just pounds of flesh. Besides, basically I just want the same thing all men do: Rice Krispies and sucking.

'Intercourse? Oh, I was around 22 or 23. Technically, that is. What is that Chinese saying? To walk a thousand miles, you first have to walk one foot. Well, to fuck a girl, you have to put one inch in. And although I'd gotten that inch in now and then, from the time I was 15, I was too afraid to leave anything as valuable as my penis in that cavern of no return.

'I don't know whether I was worried about pregnancy. I was just terrified; my repression had been so long and continuous. And, of course, there was always my foot, although I don't think that was part of the terror; although I was quite attuned to the possibility that I would have to make love in my duffel coat and snow boots, with just the offending member emerging and splurging. Emerge and splurge: the wisdom of life.

'My dread was more general: that of allowing myself to be out of control with someone I hardly knew. Which is why masturbation is always very safe, because there you not only control the person you're with, but you can leave when you want to.'

Dudley is astonishingly frank about sex, but previously has talked only briefly about his infirmity: his club foot. Well?

'When I was born, both of my feet were turned in. The right one apparently righted itself, while the left one was more severely damaged. As a result, my left leg is shorter than my right and is shrivelled from the knee down. If I look at it dispassionately, I realise it looks like a sweet child's foot. I've learned to see it that way because of the people who didn't throw up when they saw it.

'When I was a child I was constantly made aware of it. I didn't realise my foot was different until I went to school and got laughed at. My leg was an object of ridicule. Kids used to shout, "Hopalong!" and mimic me. I always wore short pants, so the greatest day in my life was when – at 13 – I was finally allowed to wear long pants and cover my leg.

'I could have been in long pants sooner, but my mother didn't want me to feel there was anything wrong – and yet she did. On the one hand, she was very anxious about my foot, and on the other, she pretended it didn't exist, which made me very confused.

'She either over-inflated me or under-inflated me. It was either "You're perfect; there's nothing wrong with you" or "You're a complete cripple." So with that came the idea that I was either a genius or a piece of crap.

'I had a very isolated youth. I was either in the hospital, being operated on, or at home, sitting in splints, recovering. I spent so much time in hospital, where the distance between me and another person was six feet, that when I finally got out in the world and was only two feet from a kid who was alive and kicking – not depressed and waiting to get well – it was suddenly very frightening. Any sense of humour I might have had was severely limited by my enormous fear of being out there.

'And I have some ghastly hospital memories. During the war, I was on a ward that was loaded with soldiers. I was the only kid. One night, there was a soldier across from me who, when they drew the curtains around him, kept screaming, "No! No! No! No!" I was very frightened.

'Later, I was wheeled into a darkened operating theatre, where I was left alone. I stayed for what seemed like two hours before anybody knew I was there. I was dying of thirst, but nobody gave me water, because nobody saw me there. Finally, this guy came in – this prick of a doctor – and said: "It's the right leg off, isn't it?" I said: "No, no, no, no. It's the left!" As it turned out, that arsehole was trying to be funny.

'Another crucial thing occurred when I was left in hospital for about two weeks without visits from my parents. My mother said she just couldn't get there, bless her heart. But I gather from psychological studies that kids up to the age of five who are institutionalised, or left on their own for more than two weeks, generally freeze up. They never quite crack out of it. I'm not sure that happened to me, but even today I'm afraid of family life. I like to be on my own, basically.

'We were poor. But so was everybody. My father was an electrician for the Stratford East Railway and, as such, he never made more than £15 a week. We didn't seem poor, but we didn't seem rich, either. Richness to me was having a bike with three speeds rather than a fixed wheel. When I did *Beyond the Fringe*, I earned in one week what my parents had managed to save in 20 years – £100.

'My father was a quiet, hidden man, whom I loved dearly but also despised because he wasn't stronger than he was. He was also a Christian Scientist, so his life was his Church – apart, of course, from the steaming, repressed sexuality that was locked inside him. My mother was an irredeemably repressed ball of floating anxiety.

'My mother was a complete fucking mess in terms of knowing who she was and what rights she had. She felt she didn't have any right to her body and, in fact, was disgusted by it. Yet, with all that, there was humour and brightness that just kept her nose above water. That – and being incredibly defensive – kept her going until she was 81.'

But what kept Dudley going as a child? Was he funny?

'No. Quite frankly, I never had any sense of humour. I was a very pompous little boy who was *driven* to humour. I got funny so I wouldn't get beaten up any more. I was bullied and pushed, mostly. See, I also liked schoolwork. So I was a hard-working kid who used to ask teachers for more work in front of other kids. I just loved to work. But, as a result, I got punished by my peer group. Once I started being funny, making fun of the teachers as they did, I was accepted.

'I stopped reading when I started clowning. I always had a vivid imagination and read like a maniac, two or three books a night. So I very much resented having to clown, because it stopped me learning and developing. Sometimes I despise the fact that I make people laugh. But being funny is a way of drawing blood without revealing where the arrow came from.

'My mother and I had a complicated relationship. We did. I was very attached to her – but very angry with her, too. She made me feel that if I made one false step, she would die. You must understand, I don't blame her for it. I don't have any bad feelings towards her now. But then she was constantly worried about my foot. My mother was obsessed by my foot and, because of that, made me obsessed by it. She had wanted to produce something perfect. My mother had a brother on whom she was quite fixated. He was a missionary in Africa and died of some disease. When she lost him, she longed to have someone to replace him. But instead of producing the perfect brother, she produced this *leg*.

'She told me she felt that way. She said the pain I was going to suffer was unbearable – but, obviously, it was the pain *she* was going to suffer, feeling, as she did, that she was on trial for producing a hunchback.

'There was nothing from her, no hugs or anything. Her excuse was that I shouldn't be touched because the plaster might break on my leg. So I often felt as if I were stuck on the mantel with a sign reading: DON'T TOUCH HIM.

'My first intimation of the effect that physical affection, particularly from a woman, had on me came from a nurse in a convalescent home. When I went into the home, I was terrified. It was my first night, and this nurse said, "Should I kiss you good night?" I said no. But then, as she was going, I said yes, and she bent down and kiss me, so loving and gentle and sweet.'

That was 'Nurse Pat' at Winifred House in Barnet, North London.

'That kiss affected my whole life. A friend said to me: "You've looked for that tenderness throughout your whole life." And I have. It haunts and sustains me. Which is why, I suppose, I live for touching and being touched.

'My mother and I never really talked about what she had done to me as a child, but there was one moment, the last time I saw her before she went into the hospital. I think she had intimations that she was about to bum off. She started bringing out old photographs, and she said: "I don't know why you say you were unhappy as a child. Look at this picture of you." And there was this picture of me smiling.

'Anyway, one Sunday afternoon, I remember saying goodbye to her, and I remember her doing what she often did: she looked at me in a peculiar, obsessive way, as if she had to put everything into it, because that was the only way she could express it – non-verbally. That particular time, I looked at her and we just nodded at each other as if to say: "Yeah, I know what we feel for each other and I know there's no way of unravelling it or somehow making good the bad parts." But in that 30 seconds, I felt as though the whole of the thing had been straightened out. And that was the last time I saw her before she went into the hospital and had an operation from which she never fully recovered.

'If I see someone with a club foot today I'm repelled. I guess because I equate it with my own repulsion about myself. It's not something I will ever be totally at ease with. In fact, my foot stops me from doing certain things. As a kid, I was very athletic, but now I do nothing, probably because I'm well-known and feel: Oh, no, I can't show *that* to people.

'With women I've always felt I had to bring up this odious skeleton, as if somehow it would fly out of bed and hit them on the head if I didn't. I always had to say "I have to tell you something. I've got this . . ."

'No woman has been unkind. Never. Never in my life. Some women, in fact, couldn't understand it at all. You know: "What are you *talking* about? So you've got a bent finger or a bent ear. What's that got to do with anything?" But even then, I wasn't convinced. I still felt I had to come up with this prologue: "Hello, I want to stick my foot up you."

'Kenny Vare first told me about sex. I was about nine or ten, and Kenny came running into the playground as if he were bearing news of the Vikings landing. "Do you know what you have to do when you grow up?" he asked. "You have to put your winkie in a girl."

'Well, by that time, having already masturbated myself into the ground, I thought: My God. I've done it. I've ruined myself for this ghastly task. I really thought there was something wrong with me.

'I've got some hilarious stories about masturbation. In fact, I've always wanted to do a film about it. I remember, through sheer fear and lust, coming six times in one evening when I was supposed to be doing my homework. I just sat there masturbating, with my parents next door. That always made things a little more titillating, you know.

'See, I had a carpet by my bed. And I used to come all

over the carpet and then rub it in. The carpet became like sculpted grass. I'll never know why on earth it was never discovered, except that my mother would occasionally say: "This carpet got all funny. Very strange, isn't it?"

'But the actual idea of masturbation never got brought up at all. Except once. We – my mother, my father, my sister and I – were all sitting around in the living room, the only room in the house, besides the bathroom, where you wouldn't freeze your balls off in winter. Anyway, Mother was sitting across the room, darning socks, while I sat on the sofa, hand in my pocket, having a nice, quiet feel. The only person watching me, as far as I could tell, was the Virgin Mary, who happened to be in a picture above our fireplace – and I knew *she* sure wasn't going to blow the whistle on me. Anyway, on the radio came a coloratura soprano, singing some Viennese piece. Suddenly, she hit an extremely high note, prompting my mother to say, without missing a beat: "This – woman – is – singing – the – highest – note – that's – ever – been – sung – don't – do – that – dear."

'Well, the moment was frozen, because my mother had discovered me. And from that night onward I could be found in the early hours of the morning frantically flipping the radio dial to find a coloratura to masturbate by. I could always come on the top note.

'Unfortunately it doesn't still work. I get a twinge, but it's just not the same thing. When I was at Oxford, however, I went into a record shop and discovered a record by someone called Mado Robin, who probably never knew what she did for me. Robin was a coloratura soprano in the French opera. On that record, she sings a B-flat in altissimo, which is, I think, the highest recorded note. Well, when I heard that, my whole body went into a fever. I thought: God, if I buy this record, I'll wank myself to death. So, instead of buying it, I used to go to the record shop, wearing my father's raincoat, slip into the glass booth and play certain cuts of the record, to which I would masturbate.

'I was wearing the raincoat. However, every time I came, I not only screwed up my face but slapped myself on the forehead – and that *did* draw considerable attention. I think the owners of the shop always wondered why I never bought the record. Finally, I did buy it and then didn't leave my room for a week. It was like a Pavlovian response – hilarious.'

From the start his lovers were beautiful women and actresses – and he explained his fascination: 'It's the fact that they compel you to look at them. Beautiful women are generally the most insecure about their looks, so they're sometimes like flashers in Central Park. They may not want to have *sex* with the whole world, but they do need to be *attractive* to the whole world.

'My first actress was intrigued that I was a virgin. I told her I'd never had an orgasm inside a woman. She said: "Oh, I think you *ought* to," and we agreed to meet in a hotel in Oxford. She came up from London on the milk train, arriving at 5 a.m. after having missed the 11 p.m. train. I was sitting on the platform waiting for her, trembling with fear, shame, anticipation and cold. We went to the hotel and got into bed. I'd rather pathetically booked us in as Mr and Mrs Moore. Can you believe that? I was so naive. It was actually fairly disastrous and the tentative preambles were not much better than the real thing. I recall looking over my shoulder at something on the wall while we were doing it. You can imagine how threatening that was.

'I found the whole thing not very exciting at all. As I came – and I'm surprised I did – she said: "Oh, I forgot to put my thing in," meaning her diaphragm. Well, she got pregnant. She told me later but said she'd deal with it and did. I saw her a couple of times after that, but it didn't work out.

'I felt a great fear in my loins – a traction of fear that shrivelled me spiritually and organically. I cringed with fear and shame and disappointment. Eventually, however, I came out of that theological funk.

'A little later I was doing *Beyond the Fringe* in London and by that time had decided that what I wanted to do with my life was perform on-stage, making people laugh and play jazz, because it attracted women. So I did that; I started playing jazz in the basement of a club called the Establishment, which Peter Cook had founded. Each night, after the performance, I'd go to play jazz and stroke girls.

'Women were the sole reason I started playing jazz. You ask any jazz musician why he wants to play jazz and he'll tell you the same thing.

'Jazz is very up-front, if you'll pardon the expression. A visceral, un-ambiguously sexual sort of music. There's an excitement to jazz that, if you understand it enough to play it, manifests itself in other areas. If you can improvise well on the keyboard, chances are you can improvise well in bed. Men who love jazz are exceptional lovers? Oh, we are. An unbeatable crowd.'

This is what the *Beyond the Fringe* mob were. Dudley fondly recalls how fame began in the Athens of the North in 1959: 'A man named John Bassett, then assistant director of the Edinburgh Festival, decided it would be a good idea to have a late-night university revue, featuring two men from Cambridge and two from Oxford, which would be presented each night after the official Festival presentation. Bassett asked me from Oxford and Jonathan Miller from Cambridge to work on it. We each recommended another person. Jonathan recommended Peter Cook and I suggested Alan Bennett. It was called The Fringe Festival. So, naturally, they wanted a fringe-type entertainment, which is why we were called *Beyond the Fringe*.

'Peter wrote most of it. Jonathan is often credited with more, but Peter was the main creative force. I'd say that on a percentage scale, starting with me at zero, Peter probably contributed 67 per cent, and Jonathan and Alan the rest. I didn't contribute a word. I provided music and did musical satires. I was intimidated by the others. Their thrust was political, social, literary, philosophical – every area I knew nothing about. The only humour I could really get into was the humour of my own background. They seemed much more knowledgeable about what was going on in the world. I didn't read the newspapers then.'

Dudley's written contributions to *Beyond the Fringe* were treated with 'benign contempt', according to Peter Cook. Dudley agrees: 'It was total scorn, thinly disguised. I just felt I couldn't contribute anything to that lot. I was always terrified that we'd get arrested for everything we did. I was very timid. I didn't know what my rights were. I came from a family that was scared of policemen, librarians, schoolteachers – everybody. There was always a feeling of not really having the right to be wherever you were at the moment. Even later, the same sense of patronising continued. Peter said: "I can't understand Dudley's success," and Jonathan said: "I think he can do better." I think they thought I'm a lightweight – doing lightweight material, having a lightweight life, lightweight hobbies and lightweight interests. Intellectual?

'I'm a performer. And there is an intellectual exercise in that. I am as intellectual as any of them in an area they don't know fuck-all about – music. To write music is an intellectual activity. Anyway, my feelings about an intellectual life are that it's the by-product of an emotional life. The intellect is the muscle growth on top of the emotional roof, instead of the other way around.

'I think I'm a terrific musician. I think I'm hot shit! I also think I'm a terrific actor and a terrific comedian. But I care more about my music than performing. Absolutely. Always have.

'I started studying piano and singing in the church choir at the age of six. From the age of 11 to 18, I used to go to London, to the Guildhall School of Music, every Saturday morning to study violin and organ. It was actually the headmaster of Guildhall who suggested I apply for an organ scholarship.

'In those days I wanted very much to please, so it seemed like a distinguished thing to do and I did. I competed in an organ-scholarship competition and won a scholarship to Magdalen College. As a working-class boy I was, indeed, greatly surprised to have been accepted. I remember the day we got the notification, my mother went absolutely wild with ecstasy. She ran down the road like Archimedes, screaming: "My son's going to Oxford!"

'I was very frightened. And when I got there, I felt very ill-equipped. Everybody spoke so factually. I had the feeling I was in the presence of very superior beings. I felt they'd all had a classical education, were older and had done national service, which I hadn't because of my leg. I felt *very* inferior.

'The toughest part of that first year was not knowing how to open my mouth without having it sound like an old saw, because, coming from Dagenham, I spoke in a very lazy accent – not Cockney but sort of suburban. I went through a terrible stage of trying to imitate other people's voices, so I ended up with a peculiar voice, very untidy, with vowels lurching in every direction. I still talk that way today.

'I was also at odds with the place, because it was too

beautiful. Magdalen College is breathtakingly beautiful. And there I was, this club-footed wanker sitting on the organ seat, playing this beautiful organ in this beautiful chapel. I felt I really didn't deserve to be there. I felt like that for two years.

'Then in my third year I started doing cabaret, and it was like being the school clown all over again. I found a niche and became rather well-known around campus as a cabaret performer, a guy who improvised and generally made a fool of himself. After that, I started acting in sketches and doing revues, which ultimately led to *Beyond the Fringe*. There were lots of good sketches but I really like the war sketch, about the so-called romance of World War Two. A lot of World War Two stories involved pilots who never returned. So in that sketch there is one scene between Peter and Jonathan in which Jonathan says: "It's up to you, Perkins. I want you to fly up to a crate, take a shufty over Bremen and don't come back!" Peter says: "Well, thank you, sir. Is this *au revoir*?" "No," replies Jonathan, "this is goodbye."'

Despite all the rumours, Dudley is adamant that: 'None of us ever used drugs then. Ever. I don't like drugs. I have no temptation. Now, I do eat a lot of sugar and salt – masses of salt. I was reading an article about people's salt consumption, and I eat twice as much as the person with the largest intake. It's probably just eating away at my balls, replacing all the sperm with sodium chloride. One day, I'll come and there'll be this little puff of salt out the end, and I'll give birth to Lot's wife.

'I did read once that salt intake gives you hardening of the penis. Now, in that case, I may double my already excessive salt intake – though, let me hasten to add, I have never had a problem with the hardening of the penis.

'I have sucked on a marijuana cigarette about a dozen times and, once, it did give me an orgasm that lasted for three days. But, then, I don't need pot, because my orgasms normally last that long, anyway.

'I've had one minor sniff of cocaine, which I did under protest, because I didn't even want to try it. Well, nothing happened. Of course, that's what everybody says. Fact is, not only do I fear being out of control, but I get a buzz from a cup of coffee; so if I took cocaine, my arse would fall to the ground, my cock would explode into 1,000 stars and a breast would turn into a cantaloupe – you know, the usual humdrum stuff.

'When *Beyond the Fringe* took off I continued living the same way I always had. I was living in a small room that cost me ten shillings a week and I stayed there. I drove a silly little car, a 1935 Austin box car, which I finally had to abandon on the side of the road. I bought another car for £40.'

After *Beyond the Fringe* ended, Dudley and Peter Cook became a team and together they presented landmark shows on stage, radio, television and film. *Not Only . . . But Also* was a hit television series for the BBC.

'The title was simple enough,' says Dudley, adding: '*Not Only Peter Cook But Also Dudley Moore*. Basically, we did the same type of comedy sketches, the same eccentric humour with some slightly smutty jokes thrown in. Well, it *was* the BBC. The BBC tried to control us, but it was a strange censorship, purely subjective.

'For instance, we once did a sketch about a confrontation between a scriptwriter and the head of the BBC. The BBC guy was saying "Listen, you can't say bloody this many times. You already said bum five times!" Finally, the writer says "All right. I'll drop bloody if you'll let me have another bum."

'The sketch was based on an actual meeting, except that at ours it was between tits and bum. We got away with tits, though I'm amazed we did. Peter *loved* it when we got away with things. Like the time he talked about a bottle of wine, which, instead of being called Château Margaux or Châteauneuf-du-Pape, was called Chat All Over the Carpet.

'Peter wrote about 70 per cent of our material and I did about 30. I used to build my humour by elaborating on things that had happened to me. Peter's came out of left field. "The Frog and the Peach", a really ridiculous sketch from the *Alice and Wonderland* segment, was from Peter's mind, all about the only restaurant left where one can find a "very big frog and a damned fine peach". The specialities of the house were frog *à la pêche* and *pêche à la* frog. Frog *à la pêche* is a frog with a peach stuck in its mouth and covered with flaming Cointreau, while *pêche à la* frog is a peach sliced down the middle to reveal hundreds of squiggling tadpoles.

'There was a take-off of James Brown's song "Papa's Got a Brand-New Bag". In the sketch, I'm supposed to be one of the great blues singers, who advertises himself as black, even though he is actually white. Naturally, I am wearing dark glasses and sitting at a piano. The name is obviously from Bo Diddley – and it's probably how Bo Derek got her name, too.

'Peter, meanwhile, plays a very upper-class BBC-type commentator, who, totally mystified by R&B, has asked me to explain the song to him, literally lyric by lyric. He says: "Now, what does this line 'Momma's got a brand-new bag' mean?" And I say: "The darky mother has gone into the bustling market streets of Harlem to purchase a gaily coloured bag." He then asks about "I'm gonna groove it, we're gonna groove it all night long." And I say: "There is some sort of celebration for the darky baby, for which the mother will be making some indentations into the bag with a groover, the work of which will take her all night long." Peter then asks about "You turn the light on for me, baby," and I explain that the baby turns the light on, blowing the circuits and causing the whole wigwam to go up in smoke.

'It is then left to Peter to paraphrase the entire song, which he does, concluding that the moral of the story can be summed up in one question: Is it wise to let people buy gaily coloured plastic bags, when they should instead have the electrical wiring redone in their houses?

'My favourite line from Peter is one that he came out

with one afternoon. We were talking about his wife and he said: "My wife does all the cooking . . . *and* all the eating. She goes down to the well every morning, but she is not a well woman." And then I said: "How did you meet your wife?" And he said: "I met her during World War Two. She blew in through the window on a piece of shrapnel and became embedded in the sofa. One thing led to another, and we were married within the hour." There's such a marvellous thoroughness about the whole thing. Very British. Somehow, he's summed up colonisation, the empire – everything – all in one go.

'Peter? He was basically, a fucking cunt. He was an enormously soft-hearted/hard-hearted, sweet/sour, vulnerable/invulnerable man. He lived on the edge of two poles. I enjoyed Peter on my own, but with somebody else we always got into an argument. We always got pissed at each other. Peter was always pissed off with my nitpicking, logical mind. And I used to get pissed off at his lack of directness in dealing with people. I don't know if you can say we split up. If something right had come along for us we would both have been delighted to do it. I felt that Peter was more interested in doing caricature stuff than in acting. He was a very funny comedian, but he's not as interested in comedic acting as I am. Right now, I just consider what I'm doing solo stuff.

'It's true, though, that after we'd taken *Good Evening* to Australia, things just ground to a halt. But we did go on to do other things, such as the Derek and Clive albums.

'Peter and I wanted to do some material we couldn't do on the radio, TV or stage. So we rented a recording studio, went in and basically improvised as we recorded. The first cut – or the first cunt, as we say in the vernacular, or the venereal – was "The Worst Job I Ever Had". Peter said: "The worst job I ever had was gettin' lobsters out of Jayne Mansfield's arsehole. Jayne used to go swimmin' off the beach at Mally-boo and these fuckin' lobsters used to go flyin' up her arse. And I used to have to pull the fuckers out."

'Again, I love that image. It's like a reversal, if you'll pardon the expression, of a cunt's having teeth. Up the arse are giant lobsters ready to get you. No matter where you stick it, you find teeth.

'In England, there are whole classes of people who talk just like Derek and Clive, whose total means of communication is in language some people call obscene. For instance, there's one cut on the album in which this bloke Pete calls me a cunt. I say back to him, in a morally outraged tone: "Who are you calling cunt, cunt?" So he says: "You cunt, *you*." I say: "You fucking cunt! You're calling me a *cunt*, you cunt?" And it just goes back and forth like that.

'What we basically did on the Derek and Clive albums was speak the unspeakable. Take, for instance, cancer, which Peter and I discuss on one album. The thing about cancer is that it's one of those subjects that, when they come up, cause everyone to put on a serious face. Everybody fears it, because we all secretly feel it's self-induced through anxiety or doubt. I know that sometimes I sink into days when I get so anxious that I conjure up an image of a white-eyed, greedy rodent gnawing away at my arsehole. *That*'s cancer-causing.

'Anyway, even though Peter and I knew that cancer was awful, it was still something we wanted to ventilate. And in doing so, we got into the most outrageous convolutions, until we ended up competing with each other over who had the worst cancer. For instance, Peter said: "I've got cancer of my wife." And I said: "That's nothing. I've got cancer of my whole fucking arse." Then he'd say: "Only that? Well listen, I've got cancer of the house." And it went on like that until we both got hysterical with laughter. As Peter says, there's absolutely no socially redeeming value about cancer, which is one of its greatest merits.

'True obscenities are not orifices. Shit and holes of the human body are not obscene, nor is making love or screwing, or whatever you want to call it. Pictures of war or violence can be obscene. You know, a woman being handed her husband in a plastic bag in Vietnam. Dreadful. And obscene.

'I remember the time I asked my mother: "What does cunt mean?" Well, she farted, snorted, her head blew off and her arms fell out. She didn't know what to do with herself. She said it was the filthiest word that had ever been invented. Imagine.

'Originally, we recorded the Derek and Clive tracks for our personal use. Copies ended up with a lot of rock groups, such as The Rolling Stones and The Who. They used to tell us they listened to them on the plane, fucking laughing their heads off. Suddenly, we thought, fuck, maybe we should release this fucking thing. Finally, we did and caused a certain small tempest in a teacup among the British press, which pretended to be self-righteous and moral. Generally, the disapproval came from those newspapers that ran a girl with bare tits on page three and talked about a vicar fucking a rooster on page four. They were the ones who objected to us boys talking dirty or calling people fucking cunts. But we got the record released and then did two others.

'I have a ribald sense of humour, what is conventionally known as obscene. It's always there and it's always been there. It's just my way of thinking. People always wonder how, with this ribald outlook, I can also write such emotional, moving music. They can't put together the feeling swings. Not to make a comparison, but Mozart had a very scatological sense of humour too. He was always talking about farts and cunts and arses. He had a very *basic* sense of humour. I don't find anything wrong with that. I just love having a fun time, cocking a snoot, as they say.

'From the time I was 13 I talked dirty. But there's a misconception that if you talk dirty, you're not a serious person. I'm very, very serious, indeed. Gosh. Absolutely. Profoundly serious. Very, very, very serious. Phew. Gosh. Golly again. Fucking A-serious.'

But what Dudley finds most serious of all – in case you haven't been paying attention – is *women*. 'I love romanticism in a woman, even though in many ways I strongly disapprove of it. I like a woman passionate and focused on me, without, of course, drifting into cannibalism. I look for someone who's huggable, has a sense of humour, a lot of feeling and can talk about the crucial things in life: enjoying yourself, dying, enjoying yourself. You know: "Oh, God, oh, God, I'm coming. Bang, pop . . . ah, done." That sort of thing.

'Brains? I don't want a woman who has anything of magnitude or devastating interest to say. Basically, I want someone to have a good time with. Fun! Smart women? Not in the slightest. Or only in the very slightest. If I want to be stirred up intellectually, I have my books and my films. It's not important to find that with the woman I'm with.

'I go for women with an overbite and flared nostrils, an aggressive, slightly hostile look. I love the looks of Bardot and Marthe Keller, both of whom have that vaguely toothy quality. Susan Anton was passionate, sensitive, full of emotions, curious and very willing to learn. But there was not an academic debate going on there. In her.

'I am not a monogamous person. I am perfectly prepared for anything. Period. I am jealous. How jealous can I be? Murder and shoving Steinways up people's arseholes.'

For someone so frank, Dudley can get annoyed when his sex life is put under too close a focus. Like the time he was supposedly having an affair with actress Elizabeth McGovern, who co-starred with him in 1983's *Lovesick*. The snag was that he was still very publicly involved with Susan Anton. He was irritated at being asked about the affair, which he denied before adding: 'What is it that people are fascinated by, anyway? Whether you put your pee-pee in somebody else's pee-pee? It's *my* business where I put my Willie Winkie – nobody else's. They can go wank themselves to death over stories about other people.' Then he made what was to be an extremely idle threat: 'I'm not going to open my fucking mouth about anything ever again.'

Give him a moment.

He kept on track: 'It's just the arid sexual lives of most people that make the supposed sexual lives of famous people interesting. The problem is that most people generally aren't doing anything except planting themselves into the vacuum system of their apartments, which I once did myself. And, Christ, it felt good. Besides, how can somebody deduce the fact that I'm having an affair with somebody because I'm talking to her at a party?'

He warmed to his theme. And despite being married four times, decided he didn't like matrimony. The main problem?

'Just *being* married. Just the notion of being married is so anathema to me that it colours my whole life. I feel starved. I feel as if I'm not available to the rest of the world – as if I have to curtail my feelings. I think being on such a monogamous level with my mother made me feel that I don't want to be married to her – or to anybody else. I've already experienced the horror and anxiety of feeling I can't move.'

But he did marry, and what about Tuesday Weld? 'I was very attracted by her waywardness, her devilishness, her unpredictability, her unbelievably aggressive humour. When I bantered with her, she always won. That was half the attraction, trying to win with her. But there was no winning, because I was afraid of her. Afraid of being rejected. And I think she knew that, even though she didn't reject me. I've always been afraid of rejection.'

His mother had rejected her sickly, underweight son at birth. She made it clear she didn't want him. She had lost her much-loved brother Billy, and Dudley was now to be the focus of her affections, but he was a disappointment. He found his first affection when 'Nurse Pat' gave him that kiss while he was in the Hertfordshire convalescent home.

'Rejection has been the primary fear of my life; therefore it's easy for me to feel in an inferior position a great deal of the time. Tuesday is very sweet and soft as butter, really. But she had weapons that she used quite devastatingly. Anybody who responds to them is finished. The main reason we finally parted was a constant locking of horns. But we're good friends and, of course, share our son, Patrick.

'I've always been terrified of children. It's not so bad now, but, frankly, I really didn't want children. Now I'm glad as Hell that I have them, but for me, the first years were not massively attractive. I'm not that sort of person. And before Patrick was born I was worried to death that he'd inherit my foot.

'There are some men who are wonderful fathers. They enjoy the years of seeing a child grow. But it's not my cup of tea, to put it in a banal way. However it's increasingly delicious. I used to think children were mainly enjoyable to women, but Patrick – well, he came, he saw, he conquered.

'I'm romantic in a way that's unreachable. My romance is out there in the dust of galaxies. That sounds so cheap, doesn't it? My God, I can even smell the ghastly perfume! My passion and romance are buried in the deep past of my youth – longing to be loved. That's the inspiration of my music. The other is sheer jest and joy.'

He says he is no longer concerned about his height – except when he puts on the pounds: 'It bothers me if I am overweight, because then I look like a fucking tennis ball. That neurosis has really faded, because every leading lady I've had has been taller. When we were doing *Six Weeks*, the first scene Mary [Tyler Moore] and I had was a party scene. She was wearing heels that none of us liked. She said: "Well, I didn't want to wear flats, in case anybody thought I was trying to accommodate Dudley's size." She didn't give a shit! Julie Andrews, on the other hand, hadn't wanted to act with me in *10* because she didn't want to act with somebody who was smaller than herself.'

As well as on-screen ladies, Dudley has had more than his share in real life. He's often indulged in what he calls 'meaningful one-night stands'. Is there a definition? 'I think you can love everybody. You can have a very deep and loving relationship with somebody . . . whom you've known two hours. Abso-bloody-lutely! If, that is, you're willing to let yourself go to the point of intimacy. I think you can have wonderful experiences with a person you've known for three minutes. I don't know that I've had that many women – only as many as I could lay my hands on.

'In terms of oral sex, I never had anybody's mouth around my nob until 1960. I was doing *Beyond the Fringe* in London and there was this girl with huge tits I was just mad for, who one day came to the theatre and said: "Dudley, I want to suck your cock." Well, there I was, 25 years old and never had it done to me. Don't ask why. But the next two years were just great. Jeez, I didn't know the delights I'd been missing. Of course, I was never keen on doing it myself but one soon realises there are results from reciprocity.

'I'm not an ardent devotee. In fact, I'm always amazed at people who wouldn't do anything else. They're probably rather favoured by women. It's probably a good enthusiasm to have.

'My own feelings about it go back to the castration complex. I'm often amazed that women can get hold of those things and pop them into their mouths. I mean, they're strange-looking creatures. If it were a bar of chocolate, I could understand. I don't think I have any taboos about it; I just haven't gone out of my way to do it. Although, I must say, I have used it to seduce women when I felt that nothing else would do the job.'

Jonathan Miller says that he and the other members

of *Beyond the Fringe* were astonished at the number of women who would go through Dudley's dressing-room as if it had a revolving door. 'I did make up for lost time. Jonathan was married, as I think Peter was. Alan didn't seem that interested in pursuing girls at that time, so that left only me. I had a marvellous time. In London, after every performance, I'd play in this club from 11 p.m. until four or five in the morning. And there were always lots of beautiful girls around. I remember one girl I was absolutely mad for, whom I never dreamed I'd be able to come to grips with. Well, I finally did, and it was such an extraordinary experience.' Why?

'I was just so turned on to her that I couldn't think of anything else. I remember one night, during a performance, I was fucking her in my dressing-room. Suddenly, I heard my cue, I was supposed to be on-stage, but I was just coming. I went "Oh my God!" and I ran down the stairs – having just come, of course – and ran onto the stage with my hair dripping wet. I looked at the others and said: "Oh, hi." They just looked at me and said hello. They knew exactly what I'd been doing. I can't think of anything in life more pleasurable than that.

'That's when I got tagged "Cuddly Dudley". And rather accurately. For me, cuddling is the most exciting thing in the world. I love it.'

Just cuddling? 'Well, I like what follows, too. I always have since it began. Marriage I don't think is the kind of thing you plan for. It's something you slide into – you know, you're looking for your dog in the back yard and suddenly you set eyes on this girl and you go aaagh! And fall into an abyss . . .

'Marriage is a commitment to the future which seems impossible to me. It's more attractive as a gesture towards a person you really enjoy being with. The commitment to being with a person until death do us part obscures the real meaning, which is to look at each moment together for itself. Confronting each second of your life rather than making a promise to be with each other until death.'

A late-starter in the sex game, Dudley always remembers the first one, the beautiful actress who took him under her wing. 'Up to then I'd always been very gauche and timid and well . . . hopeless. I'd had various tentative gropes, like the time I was with the 16-year-old French girl and we used to sneak off to the summer house and just see if anything might happen.'

He says he remains naive – but about drugs, even in the California beach culture that surrounds him. 'Honestly, I have no interest in drugs and I don't want to learn about them. I've found that people tend to be quite secretive about them once they know you have no interest, or disapprove or think it's dangerous. Which I do. The other day, a very attractive girl invited me into the toilet in a rather prim restaurant. I thought, jolly good. I'm going to get something I didn't bargain for. But she just opened her bag and offered me drugs – so I declined and went back to my lunch.

'That reminds me of the very worst thing that ever

happened to me romantically, when a girl threw up all over me, straight into my lap! It was a terrible moment. She was so embarrassed, but I was even more embarrassed for her. I never saw her again after that.'

He saw lots of others instead . . .

CHAPTER THREE

Ford to Ferrari

'Ever since I've known Dudley people have taken this "Nanny knows best" attitude to him.'

Peter Cook

His mother may have initially rejected Dudley but women were to be his salvation. Mentally. And, of course, physically. He was the one who leaned against the kitchen wall nursing a drink at those Saturday night improv parties – waiting for the girls to talk to him. The shy, timid persona was not an act at first, but when he found it worked he *worked* it.

Romantic? He was full of it. His mother knew it from the start. When he was a toddler she would tell him time and time again: 'You were born on the day Byron died 111 years ago.'

Aristocrat and poet Byron and the railwayman's son? Both had a club foot, but a strange connection to make nevertheless. In those days Dagenham had green areas, parks and trees still thriving among the concrete and the terraced houses, with their two bedrooms, living room, kitchen and – oh, the luxury – an inside *upstairs* toilet. The rent, recalls Dudley, was 'ten bob a week' – 50 pence in today's money. Not even a taxi tip.

David Russell, who in 1995 was the editor of *The Dagenham Post*, knew Dudley and his mother during the early years. 'She was a quiet, sweet women and, in her way, very determined. As a reporter for the paper, I would visit her often, especially when Dudley had some show or movie on the go. I followed his career from the very start. He was our local-lad-makes-good story. And he was always kind and helpful. He knew where he came from and wasn't going to forget it or turn his back on it. When he first started making it big he would give us stories before the national papers. He was a Dagenham lad – and he still hasn't forgotten it.

'He still attends – and, what is he now, 60? – Dagenham High School Old Boys' reunions. He's never been a turncoat to his roots. And his mother was always supportive. She used to sit with me over a cup of tea in their house – Dudley offered time and time again to buy her something bigger and better, but she would never do it – and remember the early days of Dudley and Barbara. She was a close woman, but it was clear she loved her children. I think Dudley got a tough time. He was in and out of hospital for years. There was the house and Dad and Barbara to look after, so his mother could not always be at the hospital. I think she felt guilty about it – certainly in her later years. But Dudley never seemed to complain. I think he may have felt guilty. That *he* was the problem.'

'My father was very gentle, very sweet,' says Dudley, adding: 'I would have liked to have known him better. I always regret never really spending any time with him. Now that I feel better in myself I would have liked to have taken him to lunch, whipped him off to the pub and asked him about this, that and the other. He was very timid and shy and he taught me to be not very forthcoming. I really did regret not communicating with him better.

'I was a very serious, pompous child. Well, I spent seven years of my life siphoned off in a hospital bed. I had special boots and – just like Rumpelstiltskin – the only way I could express my rage was by stamping on the floor until it collapsed and gave way. It was on my leg that I projected all my feelings of inadequacy and self-loathing.

'Now, I feel very fond of this strange lower limb that I have.

'But there are other parts of me that are quite revolted by it and keep me down. I think my mother was terrified, as people were in those days, of being laughed at and ridiculed. I'm sure that's why she wanted to kill me at birth. To have a child with a club foot, a sort of joke deformity – you know, all villains have club feet. People seemed very upset about it. Somehow there was a sort of neurotic richness about it. It was endless.'

When he was born – on Good Friday – the maternity nurse introduced him to his mother as her 'little hot cross bun'. Dudley says with a half grin-grimace: 'My mother picked me up and said: "This is not my child."' He was not the perfect replacement for her beloved brother that his mother had planned. 'When I came out mildly defective she was . . . well . . .

'People talked about it in hushed tones. With all due respect to my parents, I don't think they were massively intelligent people. They were very, very frightened of the world. The foot has caused me a lot of pain. In some ways it's been very useful. In other ways it has been harmful – in a neurotic way. It's a lifeless thing, yet it's caused me an enormous sort of combination of life and death. It's a strange enlivening thing and it's a strange mortifying thing. I've been half-driven and half-held back by it. Absolutely.

'Maybe I am always going for beauty in music, rather than beauty in women, because the music is always mildly unattainable.

'I now have this fatal flaw that I will never be able to maintain fluidity in the way I play because there is a lack of fluidity in me as a person, as it were. In my physical self. It may all be a reflection of that.

'It's like my height. I sometimes forget how small I am until I see myself in a shop window, but it doesn't bother me. It used to a great deal. In the days when self-esteem was at a premium, I used to feel a little nervous about myself – not feeling I could do this or that because of my height.'

Most of that hurt and doubt began in Dagenham. It was a London overspill community, but *community* is a kind word to use. In the newspaper land of London's Fleet Street, Hell was defined as covering a motor industry strike 'in Dagenham on a rainy day'.

For Dudley, it represented other sorts of Hell. This was a land of 'lads' and flat surfaces and football. It was a working-class jungle of recently set concrete and solidly cemented prejudice, where Dudley remembers everybody was 'bigger and shittier than I was'. Dagenham in the 1930s was not a place where the out-of-the-ordinary was tolerated, let alone understood. Every peer group strived to mirror itself. And what do you do with a funny foot? Lots of jokes, of course. But they came later.

'When I was a kid of about 13 I was made aware I was small, and I felt a bit strange about it, but now it's of no consequence.' Of his foot he says: 'Mine was a severe case, but it has never stopped me doing anything. I have my boots made so I balance – otherwise my legs get very tired.'

Custom-made boots and all the other trappings of success seemed remote from Dudley's childhood home at 14 Monmouth Road, in the south of Dagenham's Becontree Estate. It lay close to Dagenham County High School – now the Sydney Russel High School, after the educationalist who took a great interest in his boys – which Dudley attended in his black, blue and white uniform after passing his Eleven Plus in 1946. He and his sister Barbara were not war evacuees, but instead were 'bombed out' of Monmouth Road after half a dozen German grenades fell on the street.

The family were moved to 146 Barron Road, which offered almost identical accommodation, where his parents were to live until their deaths, his father in 1971 and his mother a decade later. His parents had been supportive of Dudley. At Dagenham Primary School the teachers advised that he should go to a special school to deal with his infirmity.

'My mother did her piece,' recalls Dudley's sister Barbara. 'As far as she was concerned, Dudley was normal. There was nothing wrong with him. That was my mum's attitude. And, as it turned out, she was right.' But Dudley's foot never was, despite the seven years of surgery that began when he was only two weeks old.

Dagenham County High catered for both boys and girls, but 'playtime' was segregrated. Dora Williams was the daunting headmistress for Dudley's tenure and she inadvertently helped him by establishing a school choir and launching drama and music festivals every two years. He was an aggressive bookworm, which did not win any points with his classmates. Here was this short, limp-along boy who *wanted* to work. His attitude was not a popularity-contest winner.

His music was. His mother was an accomplished player and she urged her children to learn. Barbara had taken lessons from the age of four. Dudley wanted to play the violin, but his mother cautioned that it would be better to learn the basics of the piano first. 'She was very proud of how well Dudley did musically,' remembers David Russell, adding: 'I don't think she ever thought he would accomplish what he has done in music. He got his interest in music from her and he's always enjoyed it. It's like all these things – if you are good at something you tend to pursue it.'

Apart from female figures, the young Dudley also liked arithmetic tables. He was clever at mathematics and in his growing years saw himself as a teacher in the subject. But he had a musical talent that overtook other ambitions.

His music teacher, Peter Cork, with whom he went on a walking tour of the Lake District, maintains: 'His abilities were quite extraordinary. He had a remarkable talent. I don't think there was any question about what he should devote his studies to. He was, and is, gifted.'

It was Dudley's passport from Dagenham – an inherited talent, which his family thought might have been handed down from a distant relative who met his end with the 'Charge of the Light Brigade'.

Dudley himself was certainly to take a blind run at life. He disguised his insecurities and his minimal self-esteem with clothes, cars and girls. But, in time, his work – the music, the comedy and the acting – made him an all-round entertainer, although all the success could not cloak, never mind drive away, the demons that haunt him still.

But as a working-class 'lad' in Dagenham he wanted to be liked. 'By the time I got to school I was primed to be bullied, not so much because of my size but my temperament. I was very good at my studies, but one day I decided to abandon the academic life and make them laugh before they laughed at me. It might be the road to ruin but it was better than any other. There I was, top lad, and I dropped to eighth. I took up music as a main subject because I knew I wouldn't have to work at it.'

His studies suffered from him 'being one of the boys'. He would make jokes and remarks, often turning on himself and his height for the humour. ('Being short is good for comedy,' he would declare later.) No longer top-of-the-class, he found his new status favoured by his classmates. Since then he has always wanted to be the centre of attention. And he doesn't hide his annoyance if he's not. Centre-stage via music and laughter is where he feels 'on' and most comfortable.

The comedy he most liked was on the 'wireless'. He was listening to *The Goon Show* and *Around the Horne* and Peter Sellers, Harry Secombe, Michael Bentine and Spike Milligan – 'The Goons' – made him understand the joy and amusement that could be derived from the absurd; from the ridiculous; from left field. He and, later, Prince Charles were ardent fans. It was also a lesson for Dudley about what could be done with an ensemble. The burden was not just on one performer but was spread around – as, of course, was the pressure.

Dudley never liked pressure. But he sought it. And found it.

It happened at first at a scholastic level. He won a scholarship to the Guildhall School of Music and Drama, which is now based in London's Barbican. There he received intellectual instruction – he said he read music like detective stories, anxious to see what was on the next page – as well as practical, learning the violin, at last, and the organ. His voice was also trained.

This was 'Saturday school' and it was not a long trip from the East End to Blackfriars, where the Guildhall was then situated. Dudley impressed his tutors with his instinctive touch and love of music. He could read it like a novel. He sweated through from Monday to Friday waiting for his weekend class. A wizard on the piano, he was, as he says, nevertheless persuaded to try for a university organ scholarship. He was told to go for the best. He tried for Cambridge but says his nerves got the better of him.

Instead, he was accepted by Magdalen College, Oxford, a grand and historical seat of learning with centuries of history and accomplishment. Dudley's 'interview' could have been taken straight from *Monty Python*. His left leg was too short to put enough pressure on the organ pedals. With his specially made shoes he was able to play cricket and kick a ball around, but the organ pedals did present a problem, as he needed more elevation. His solution was to take an old shoe of his mother's, build an extra heel onto it, cut a groove in the sole and strap on the shoe, so that his toes were pulled up to an angle at which he could forcefully tread the pedals.

'It was an extraordinary-looking thing,' he recalled. 'I remember going for my organ scholarship and saying: "Will you excuse me? I just have to put this contraption on." And out comes this old brown shoe of my mother's, with this bootlace tied round the back of my leg. I was very self-conscious about my foot, and for me to do that was an indication of how much I wanted to get into university.'

The committee of dons sitting in judgement approved his application and in October 1954 the Dagenham 'lad' was a student at one of the most prestigious colleges in the world.

It was a scholastic triumph, but initially a social disaster. 'I felt dwarfed, if you'll pardon the expression, by the social ease of the people who'd come from public schools.'

Jonathan Hews, who produced Dudley's two classical music series for Channel 4, *Concerto* and *Orchestra*, said: 'When Dudley went to Oxford he felt he was a bit of an impostor coming from the very humble two-up, two-down that was his childhood home in Dagenham. He was wracked with self-doubt, and still is, but he suddenly discovered that, almost because of his humble view of himself, women found him incredibly attractive. So he rode his luck and tried picking up the tallest girls at university because it was so ridiculous. And to his surprise it worked.'

It kept on working years later. Tom Mankiewicz, son of legendary film-maker Joseph L. Mankiewicz and himself a screenwriter and director with credits including some of the 1970s' Bond films, is an affable man. He and Dudley have been long-time friends. One year Mankiewicz was staying at the then prime Hawaiian hotel, the Kahala Hilton on Oahu, as were Dudley and the present tall blonde in his life, Susan Anton.

'One day I suddenly saw in real life what Dudley is all about. There were two figures on the beach strolling hand-in-hand into the water in the sunset – Dudley and Susan Anton. As I watched them they walked deeper and deeper into the water, and suddenly the waves were right up to Dudley's neck while they were still lapping around Susan's thighs. As a comic image you could not get anything funnier.'

But at Oxford Dudley was a musical hit. With his special boot for his left foot, he impressed everyone with his skill, dedication and courage. Especially Bernard Rose, his musical tutor, who was to become a lifelong friend. Indeed, the majority of Dudley's friends and associates have remained on good terms with him – even his former wives.

Rose admired Dudley's 'imagination' as well as his love for music. But his pupil was also getting more sociable. He lived for a time in Grammar Hall, one of those Oxford buildings you expect Colin Dexter's Inspector Morse to wander through, making discreet enquiries.

It was a fine place for parties. And there were many. Dudley played piano at one gathering that honoured tragic actress Dorothy Dandridge – then lauded as the star of 1954's *Carmen Jones*, she was later discarded by Hollywood and died still waiting for another starring role – and Lord Snowdon, then Tony Armstrong-Jones, took the photographs. It was Dudley's showcase. He was good. He knew it. And soon the whole college did, especially through Anthony Page, who also lodged at Grammar Hall and was to play a pivotal role in the professional development of Dudley.

Page cast him as Enobarbus in a production of *Antony and Cleopatra*. Bernard Rose had told Dudley it would be in his interests to work full out for a First-Class degree (he finally got a Second in 1957). But he was stage-struck: 'The stage had beckoned: revue, cabaret women. All I'd ever seen was *Bless the Bride* with my parents, though we went to the cinema. I remember seeing *Red River* with John Wayne at the Mayfair cinema in Dagenham and it was so foggy the fog came in and you couldn't see the screen.'

But acting or not, Dudley kept coming back to music. He played jazz in the clubs – 'it got the girls' eyes sparkling sooner than preludes and fugues and that was all I was interested in' – and composed music for theatrical productions, recording the organ and piano at Magdalen Chapel. This talent for writing theatrical scores would take his music and him to the movies.

He left Oxford in 1958, having stayed on for his music studies, following a landmark Commemoration Ball, which boasted Johnny Dankworth and his wife Cleo Laine as the main attraction. Dudley also performed, to a string of ovations. The Dankworths were so impressed that they told Dudley that when they next had a vacancy in the band he had the job.

Dudley didn't want to wait. 'Then I remembered,' says Dankworth, 'that there was an opportunity for a pianist.' And so Dudley ended up with an interview with Vic Lewis, who fronted the Vic Lewis Band, which was one of Britain's most popular touring bands in the early 1950s.

It was to become his first job. His pay was £40 a week. It was a great opportunity. Nat King Cole and

Johnny Ray had performed with the Vic Lewis Band. Lewis says that Dudley was a born soloist – even when other band members were doing their solo. It is the number-one sin in a band to play solo when someone else is. Dudley did so but Lewis comments: 'If he had been a nasty little character he wouldn't have lasted long. But everyone loved him.'

It has been a frequent comment throughout his life.

American and British musicians had by the mid-1950s – much of the successful negotiations being credited to Vic Lewis, who would later manage stars like Shirley Bassey – arranged an exchange deal. One band from Britain would tour the United States and vice-versa. In early 1959 Count Basie was on his way to Britain, and the Vic Lewis Band, with their new piano player, were *en route* to America. 'It was my first trip – it was because of Vic that I came to America,' Dudley fondly recalled many years later, adding: 'I was in a constant state of happiness. We played Army and Navy bases on the East Coast. California? It didn't mean anything then. The money (£100 a week), the girls and the drinks were big.' It was an intoxicating mix.

But all good things end. The tour over, most of the band returned to their families. Dudley and Lewis hung around New York, staying at a hotel near the bright lights of Broadway. Dudley teamed up with three other musicians and formed the Moore Jazz Combo. They got a booking at the Village Vanguard nightclub in Manhattan, and Dudley soon became the star of the show, not just in name but in performance. Ahmet Ertegun of Atlantic Records heard Dudley play and offered him a recording contract.

But Dudley's self-confidence was not up to it. He was still the 'lad', and America and the thought of being 'found out' – believing his talents were not great enough to compete in this land of jazz – frightened him. Home and familiar faces and surroundings felt like a better idea. Back in Britain he joined up again with Vic Lewis in London. But it was a short reunion. Dudley yearned for more time in the spotlight, centre-stage. He got in touch with Johnny Dankworth, who immediately agreed that he could join the John Dankworth Band. Dudley played for his supper, and everything else, diligently for nine months. 'I was a bit nervous about playing behind the soloists, because at that time I was on a great Errol Garner kick. I played in his style, even when other musicians were trying to make a chorus, and they felt it was impossible to solo against me. It helped my confidence.'

So much so that he formed his own act – the piano with gags and one-liners. Clowning and music. To him it seemed an obvious winner. He started in clubs around Dagenham. It was a low point for Dudley. At one club he was signed up with wrestlers and strippers. He was on after the fights and the bouncing girls. 'No one warned me what a dive it was. So after the strippers went off, I came out and did a brilliant satire on Schubert's *Lieder* and some of the more obscure operas of Benjamin Britten!'

Dudley's heart – and future – was not in being a Victor Borge for the working-class.

And so began the Dudley Moore Trio. He was joined by Hugo Boyd on bass and Derek Hogg on drums. They worked well together and became a popular act as 1959 turned into the Sixties – a tumultuous decade for Dudley, as it was for much of the world. But Boyd, who worked as an architect before joining Dudley, was killed in a car crash in the South of France. With a friend who was also an architect he was driving along the Corniche when his car went out of control and spun off the road, crashing down a hill to the railway tracks below. In one of those stranger-than-fiction moments, the car hit the tracks just as a train approached and shoved it more than 100 yards before being able to stop. By then both young men were dead.

'It hurt Dudley a lot', recalls David Russell, adding: 'They were good friends – Dudley's best friend really – and Dudley took the accident very badly. He went into deep depressions about it. It all seemed so unfair. A young talent just making it. And of course it was tragic.'

Hugo Boyd's funeral took place at the crematorium in Golders Green in North London. Dudley played the organ. 'I've played for weddings and funerals. It's always hard, for you want to be perfect for both the living and the dead. Hugo had been a good friend and it wasn't easy. But I felt he was there as I played. Hugo had gone but his spirit was with us. Still is.'

In time the group re-formed, with Australian Peter McGurk on bass, replacing Hugo Boyd, and Chris

Karan, another Aussie, taking over from Derek Hogg on drums. Karan was penniless when he got the job and remembers: 'I went to sit on a session with Dudley at The Establishment. The moment we started to play it was magic. And at five in the morning Dudley was telling me how great it was to have found the right drummer at last. As I didn't have a bean I asked if I could have a week's wages in advance. He gave me £20 straight away and when I went to pay it back a week later he didn't want to know about it. He's always been enormously generous to people around him – and not just with money. Just by helping people out in other ways, by talking and being with you. He would always listen.'

This particular Dudley Moore Trio made three jazz albums together and recorded the sound track for *30 Is a Dangerous Age, Cynthia*. They were a strong attraction for seven years until it all went tragically wrong. McGurk became emotionally distraught as his girlfriend Heather fell in love with and married Karan. McGurk was found dead from a drugs overdose at his first-floor apartment in London's Putney in 1968. There were half a dozen letters – the contents have never been publicly revealed – that convinced coroner Gavin Thurston not to hesitate in delivering a verdict of suicide.

Dudley talked about 'a jinx' on his bass players. He could not understand what so troubled McGurk. That desperate need to be loved by one special person. It is, and remains, one of the quests in his own life.

It was some time before the group re-formed, first with Jeff Clyne and later with Pete Morgan, and they were still recording a decade later.

McGurk had killed himself three days after Dudley's wedding to Suzy Kendall in Hampstead. It was a horrid start to a honeymoon, and to a marriage.

By then Dudley was a big name in Britain. *Beyond the Fringe* had been a huge international success; he had made a couple of movies as well as lots of music, including incidental music for two plays at London's Royal Court; and he had been working with the Royal Shakespeare Company. He wrote film scores for legendary director Stanley Donen's *Staircase* in 1968 and for Anthony Page's classic movie *Inadmissible Evidence*, starring Nicol Williamson, a year earlier. Along the way there were commercial jingles for soap powder and orange juice, and a reworking of the music for *Swan Lake*, as well as lots of composing and creating. 'Even if I'm in some silly flat and I see a piano I want to play it,' he said at the time. Dudley also inspired the brilliant dancer Gillian Lynne, who is now one of Britain's best-regarded stage and screen dance directors, who counts *Cats* among her long-lasting accomplishments. She credits him with teaching her about rhythm in jazz and calls him 'the most important influence of my life'. So few people, she said, have a gift for jazz and classical music that 'It was a tragedy that he stopped composing and became a star.'

Dudley may reflect on that. But star he most certainly was in 'Swinging Sixties' Britain.

But Judy Scott-Fox, who was then Peter Cook's personal assistant and is now a talent agent in Los Angeles, said: 'Dudley didn't seem to know what he wanted out of life. He was always curled up in a corner *not* talking.'

The *Beyond the Fringe* team of Dudley, Cook, Miller and Bennett had by then been well established. Author Glenys Roberts, who was an intimate part of their circle, agrees with Scott-Fox: 'That is exactly how I first remember Dudley myself. Two graduate students had taken on the lease of an abandoned pub in Cambridge, which became a literary salon for the alternative society. It was there I met Cook, who kept a room there with Wendy (Snowden), an art student who became his first wife, and he introduced me to the rest of the team. As it happens, the foursome were not only neatly divided between universities of Oxford and Cambridge, they also lined up on either side of the still-lingering chasm of the British class system. Cook and Miller, sons of privilege, would peak early. Moore and Bennett, the scholarship boys from the sticks, would take their time finding their way in the world, but now that they have done so it is to greater acclaim.

'This is difficult for anyone to handle, but it was most difficult of all for Cook, who was closest to Moore professionally.'

The tall, angular Cook always appeared the dominant half of their enduring partnership. People did indulge a 'Nanny complex' towards Dudley. 'He's always been latched onto by other people trying to make him do what *they* want,' said Scott-Fox, adding: 'He never appeared to have any plans, but when someone cast him in the role of *their* making, he always came up trumps.'

An all-round talent, a star, but not the instantly recognisable one he was to become. There is a wonderful story of Sir John Gielgud meeting Dudley in a private lounge at London's Heathrow Airport. The man who was to star in one of Dudley's most popular films and appear in its sequel, when told that Dudley was off on holiday to Portofino in Italy, said to the young performer: 'Darling, you must look up my friends Rex Harrison and Lilli Palmer, who have a home there. I will write a note introducing you.' When it was read out at the elegant Harrison home overlooking the Gulf of Genoa, what Gielgud had written was revealed: 'Darling Rexie, This is to introduce the brilliant young accordionist Stanley Moon.'

This hurt, but Stanley Moon was thereafter established as Dudley's *alter ego* and would be the name of his character in *Bedazzled*. In the 1990s he would have liked some anonymity: 'I don't lead a normal life. The more I'm known, I never go out and expose myself, because with the advent of cable and stuff and the older you get, there is just the *weight* of recognition that builds up over the years.' Nevertheless, Dudley was always ready for his close-up, just like Norma Desmond in *Sunset Boulevard*.

By the late Sixties Dudley was living in Hampstead with Suzy Kendall. British actress Fiona Lewis, who now lives and writes scripts in Hollywood, says: 'Even in those days Dudley and Suzy had a remarkable lifestyle. They had a secretary and a Ferrari before anyone else did. It was clear they intended to go places.'

Dudley had already make quite a journey from the land of Ford to Ferrari society.

And this was just the beginning.

CHAPTER FOUR

Cuddly Dudley

'Men always think girls go for gorillas. In fact, they like gentle, sweet men like Dudley.'

Hollywood agent Jo Lustig

The Sixties seemed to have been created for Dudley, who happily and flagrantly indulged in his passion for women and music. He was an energetic elf. He steadily worked his way through the decade. The evenings were spent performing *Beyond the Fringe* and after 11 p.m. he would be at the Establishment Club – Peter Cook's self-styled 'London's First Satirical Nightclub' in Soho's Greek Street – playing piano and grinning at the girls. Eventually one would be bundled into his Mini-Cooper – in 1995 he still kept it in a North London garage – and they would whizz off to the one-bedroom apartment he was renting from Johnny Dankworth in the London suburb of Kilburn.

Music and sex, and vice-versa, was the mantra. They comprised his orchestra and he was the conductor.

He may not have been a fan of cunnilingus but the reverse was always acceptable, and there were some madcap early morning drives through the streets of London when he had one hand on the steering wheel and the other one slapping his forehead, as a girl's head bobbed between his legs.

But *Beyond the Fringe* was *serious* business. In 1959–60 John Bassett was working as assistant to Robert Ponsonby, who had the position of artistic director of the Edinburgh Festival. Ponsonby was in charge of an Arts extravaganza which – unlike the Festival dominated by stand-up comics desperate to be seen by television talent 'scouts' that emerged in the 1990s – was crushed with breakthrough talent. Some of it was raw, blue meat. 'He wanted to expand it – to put some "professionals" on-stage. The Fringe then was two boys and a top hat sometimes. There could be some great shows but often there was not much to see,' says Richard Mowe, who in 1995 was Arts Editor of *Scotland on Sunday*. He added: 'It was an Establishment thing in a strange way. They wanted the Fringe to be a success, so the official Festival sponsored its own off-the-wall show. It wasn't the Fringe. And it wasn't the mainstream Festival. That's why they called it "Beyond the Fringe".'

Oxford man and jazz devotee Bassett knew all about Dudley's talents. He was also acquainted with Alan Bennett – Dudley's Oxford contemporary, who still looks like an absent-minded don, albeit one of the century's great writing talents – who had gone with the Oxford Theatre Group to Edinburgh in 1959 with *Better Late*. He knew Jonathan Miller even better. Peter Cook related how the landmark, star-making show began. It's typical Cooky.

'He [Bassett] was looking for a late-night revue. They'd had Flanders and Swann the year before. And he knew Dudley personally, he knew Jonathan and he'd heard of me. In fact, he asked Jonathan to suggest two other people – one from Oxford and another from Cambridge. Jonathan suggested me. Dudley mentioned Alan. I was the only one with an agent (and a tailor). He advised me against doing the show. He said it would be an amateur revue and I'd spoil my status as a professional. I finally decided to do it anyway. The others were to get £100 to do it, but my agent insisted that I get more. So I got £110. My agent took 10 per cent leaving me with £99.'

If any of them could have imagined what was to result from this they would have held out for thousands and thousands of pounds. *Beyond the Fringe* was the start of the satirical Sixties. David Frost and *That Was The Week That Was*, and later the *Monty Python* crew as well as many single, double and group acts that followed, were inspired and sparked-off by Dudley and his colleagues.

Alan Bennett was studying Russian history at Oxford when he was rounded up for the revue. By the late 1990s – getting on for 40 years after his success with *Beyond the Fringe* – he had written stunning plays like *Forty Years On*, *The Old Country*, *Enjoy*, *Kafka's Dick* and television plays, like the classic *An Englishman Abroad* with Alan Bates and the late Coral Browne. His play *The Madness of King George III* was turned into a film as *The Madness of King George*. Hollywood thought movie-goers might think 'George III' was a sequel and wonder why they had never seen or heard of the previous two films. It was a spectacular success, winning

Oscar nominations for stars Nigel Hawthorne and Helen Mirren. Bennett – who also did a series of monologues entitled *Talking Heads* and *A Question of Attribution* – published *Writing Home* in 1994, a compilation of his diaries from 1980 to 1990. It was an instant bestseller. And a classic.

Jonathan Miller was a qualified doctor and wit. At Cambridge he studied neuropathology, but on-stage his work and vision have been eclectic. He presented the BBC series *The Body in Question*, as well as doing Shakespeare, he's lectured, produced and directed shows and opera, including *The Mikado*, an opera with – surprise, surprise! – Dudley Moore, who appeared in it wearing exquisite evening dress in Los Angeles in 1988.

Miller was 'the intellectual' but he was also sought-after by theatre groups following student shows like *Out of the Blue* in 1954 and *Between the Lines* a year later. He wasn't sure whether to follow medicine or entertainment. In the end, he has had a colourful and creditable career bridging the gap.

Dudley was the jazzman. Peter Cook was the other professional, having written several shows, including the London West End offering *Pieces of Eight*. Dudley said of him after several years of collaboration: 'I cannot conceive of working with someone with a more royally precise sense of timing and character.' Of course they spent many years together calling each other 'You cunt!' or alternatively 'You fucking cunt' – and that wasn't just in their 'blue' Derek and Clive recordings. It was, in effect, a love affair. Pete 'n' Dud were a team. Old footage of television talk shows with them reflects the camaraderie, the joy and the plain fun they could get from, and give, each other. Cook was tall and good-looking – just like Dudley's girlfriends and wives.

But when John Bassett brought the quartet of talent together they 'disliked each other on sight', according to him. They all believed they were 'stars'. Solo performers. What was this ensemble thing? Dudley, of course, remembered 'The Goons'. Not surprisingly, so did the others. This *could* work.

It did.

At the Royal Lyceum Theatre in Edinburgh, which stands adjacent to the Usher Hall, the venue for all the Festival's 'upmarket' presentations, and a short walk from city landmarks like Princess Street Gardens and Edinburgh Castle, *Beyond the Fringe* began on 22 August 1960. It was meant to begin at 10.45 p.m. But 'some kid' got the timing a little late and history began five minutes later.

Media producer David Gibsone, who was a teenager in 1960, remembers: 'My father had taken me to the show. We were lucky to get tickets but he was an entertainment writer for a Scottish newspaper and had a bit of influence. We had read nothing but rave reviews, but you normally take them with a pinch of salt. The theatre was very hot and we were very uncomfortable. The house lights dimmed and the discomfort vanished. For some reason I remember Alan Bennett more than the others. Everything they did seemed to be so anti-establishment and irreverent. I was only 13 but I knew that this was different. People were literally falling about in their seats. Their show had 'it' – whatever it is. Occasionally you see a play or a TV show or a movie that you know is something special. *Beyond the Fringe* was special.

'Dudley was the music man and the others worked with the words. It was obvious from the start that this was an impressive act. Something that was going places. They delivered the laughs again and again. My father, who had been to so many of these first nights, couldn't stop talking about *Beyond the Fringe*. It was, he said, a winner.'

Mr Jack Gibsone was, as usual, correct.

But Dudley felt uncomfortable. This was a world for which his background had not prepared him. The past has always been part of his present. Here were these three tall men, who seemed to tower over him, not just physically but intellectually. He was the music man where they were the writers – especially Peter Cook, who all his life could find amusement in the air he breathed. His life comprised one-liners. Cook never accommodated Dudley's anxiety. He helped him by just brushing it aside with remarks like 'you fucking club-footed dwarf'. Not a politically correct devotee, was Cook. The others were more careful. Alan Bennett, who had looked so sad and withdrawn at Peter Cook's memorial service, said that Dudley didn't so much create the words but 'perfectly clowned them'.

Bennett, who can make commas dance, felt that

Dudley was wary of words. And he was: 'It was difficult for me with these guys. They seemed to know so much more and they could make jokes out of the air. They seemed grown-up – and I don't mean that in a funny way. They just seemed to be "people". I did feel a little humiliated by them. Humbled, if you like.'

It may have been daunting, but the challenge did not deter him. All his life Dudley has found himself the odd-man-out, but he has usually triumphed in his David/Goliath contests. He could cope with 'dolly birds' and the same evening with an inventive reworking of 'Colonel Bogey' – which involved Beethoven's Fifth, which on-stage had Dudley playing perfectly but then, to increasing laughter, unable to finish the piece. Not a man for homework, Dudley prefers 'instant inspiration' and it worked, and continues to work for him.

Beyond the Fringe ran for just under (but more likely just over) an hour and involved the group in sketches, monologues and music. They fine-tuned it as they went along. It just got better and better.

When the show opened, after week-long runs in Cambridge and Brighton, at the Fortune Theatre in London, on 10 May 1961 – the same year Peter Cook started *Private Eye* – the pot-pourri of social comment, craziness, daftness and, in those days, outlandish lampooning diatribes at everything from the monarchy to strategic weapons touched the nerve of the nation. *Beyond the Fringe* was not just a hit: it was a sensation. A one-of-a-kind.

The oddball quartet from Oxbridge were stars. And

Dudley loved it. Once again he was centre-stage. All over the place.

He was starring in *Beyond the Fringe*, was the star attraction in Soho at The Establishment, *and* he was asked to write the music for the Western Theatre Ballet's *The Owl and the Pussycat*, a one-act ballet based on the poem. Gillian Lynne was the choreographer. They became something of a team and were asked to work on *England, Our England*, a revue written by that other talented twosome, Keith Waterhouse and Willis Hall. The idea – the contrast between the North and South of England – was strong, as was the cast: Billie Whitelaw, Roy Kinnear and Bryan Pringle. Reasonably popular out-of-town, it was not however a great success when it reached the Shaftesbury Theatre – in 1961 called the Princess Theatre – in London. Nevertheless, a poster for the show has a prominent place on the staircase wall of Billie Whitelaw's Suffolk cottage.

Whitelaw, Irish writer Samuel Beckett's muse for quarter of a century and one of Britain's longest-serving actresses on stage, film, television and radio, laughs about the chaos of the production. The original director, Reggie Smith, was replaced for turning up rather tired and emotional from drink. Director John Dexter, who had a reputation as a tough operator, was called in. 'I nearly didn't do the show,' remembers Billie Whitelaw, adding: 'I was so gripped by panic.'

Dudley was relaxed. 'I remember him singing and dictating a song down the phone to me. It was to be used on-stage the next day. And here he was presenting it to me on the telephone. It was crazy but it worked. Everyone adored Dudders. They were silly, crazy, wonderful times. And Dudders has done well.'

So, of course, had *Beyond the Fringe*. Dudley was in America with the revue when he and Gillian Lynne were asked to work on the jazz ballet *Collages* for the 1963 Edinburgh Festival. In New York he recorded the music and air-freighted the tapes. As America applauded *Beyond the Fringe* he was getting more and more commissions to provide show music.

And was falling in and out of love. Nightly. Daily.

'In the Sixties I had quite a run in the sexual sense. It was funny when they started calling me a "sex symbol" after *10* because, in all modesty, that sort of thing happened in England in the Sixties. In *10* George Webber spent all his time looking for the perfect woman and I think men identify with that. I've run after "10s" all my life.

'I started getting interested in girls when I was nine or ten years old. That's normal, isn't it? But I used to have a very oblique approach to courting. At 14 I fell in love with a girl called Shirley Powell, a blonde. She used to wear stripy sweaters. I couldn't say boo to her . . . I was living in Dagenham and she lived about ten miles away in Rainham. My courting technique was to get a friend to go with me and we'd play football outside her house for about two hours, hoping she'd come out. She never did. So once I threw a ball over the back garden and knocked at the door.

'She came to the door, I pretended I didn't know her

and asked for my ball back. She went inside for about five minutes looking for the ball, and said she couldn't find it. I said: "Oh, thank you." And left. We never did find the ball.

'That was my courting pattern years ago. I think it's improved a bit since then. I've married women other men might regard as "10s". I've been madly in love too. I was in Australia and fell madly in love with an Australian reporter. She was very, very young, really lovely. I was on tour and had gone home to England, but after a week I flew out to Australia again to see her. It was all very hush-hush. I was quite well-known out there and spent a couple of weeks hiding out in a little apartment. Very romantic.

'I'm not chauvinistic. I like women but I never know what fascinates me about them until it's there. It's a combination of things – physical attraction and humour. I like a woman who has a lot of humour.'

What he doesn't like are male predators. With disdain and distaste he tells the story of Erik Estrada, the Latin-looking actor who won much popularity on the American television series about Californian motorcycle cops *CHiPs*. 'He came into the room, wandered over to a tall Swedish girl, looked her over like a meat salesman, gave a leering wink and said: "Big girl, love it" and swaggered off.'

Not Dudley Moore's style at all. His friend George Hastings, with whom he 'lodged' while between wives and affairs, once said of him: 'He is one of the nicest people I have ever known.'

Nice. But always confused.

In 1960 he was involved with blonde actress and model Anna Leroy – a cleavage-clocking, statuesque Brogan Lane lookalike – who was appearing in Lionel Bart's *Oliver!* but their relationship was the first of many that collapsed because Dudley felt, as he puts it, 'too hemmed in'.

The 'dolly birds' were everywhere. Dudley met them all. There was Penny Farah, who was close to another rising star, Michael Caine. George Hastings introduced him to girls like Rosemary Bond and her sister Patsy. But it was Celia Hammond, who in the 1990s we would call a 'supermodel', who really got Dudley's 'juices flowing'. She made a cameo appearance typecast as a seductive beauty opposite Sean Connery's James Bond in *Goldfinger* in 1964.

Celia Hammond and Jean Shrimpton – both Lucy Clayton model-agency graduates – were *the* faces and figures of the early 1960s.

Dudley Moore was also beginning to be one. He and Hammond, then 21, met at the Establishment Club as he sat playing magic on the piano. It was lust at first sight and then later, for Dudley at least, a deep, almost obsessive love. She had arrived with cult photographer Terence Donovan (later and briefly the actress Patsy Kensit's father-in-law) and left with him. But Dudley was smitten. And Celia Hammond was interested. Their friends got them together and they were a Sixties chemistry set. She adored music. He adored her. The perfect formula.

Their inseparable infatuation ran for a year.

But then Dudley was in New York with *Beyond the Fringe*. He would call her. There would be no answer. He would check the time. Where was she? Out with someone else? Worse still, in bed with someone else? His insecurities increased by the moment and he just sat by the telephone, calling and calling. He would punctuate calls to his model woman with calls to friends and would jabber on endlessly about the love of his life.

In New York Dudley was living in a roomy apartment offered to him by the singer and actress Joan Diener, another of his growing host of fans. He asked Hammond to join him. Looking around at the library of letters she had received from Dudley and thinking of the expensive hours spent on the phone, she agreed to be with him for a few weeks.

John Bassett was staying with Dudley and was asked to help in an experiment. Bassett would be in one room and Dudley and his love in another. Dudley shut all the doors, got on his bed and then made hilarious lovemaking sounds to see if Bassett could hear the action when Hammond arrived. Bassett assured his lovelorn – and increasingly randy – friend that all would be tranquil.

As far as sex and noise went, all was well.

'He was a jazz pianist in a nightclub and a friend introduced us' is how Celia Hammond remembers the romance 30 years later. 'The whole thing happened very quickly. Dudley was off to work in America so I went there with him. He is the easiest person in the world to be with – he couldn't have been more accommodating and pleasant. I don't know why he says he's difficult to live with. Perhaps because none of his relationships have worked out he is putting the blame on himself.

'I was his first well-known girlfriend. I didn't spot the pattern of tall blondes with long hair at the time. I found him extremely attractive and his height had nothing to do with it. He was the perfect gentleman.

'He's a man that loves women, which always makes a woman feel special. He was also shy, which is endearing.

'Right from the start I really thought he was incredibly attractive. He's got very mischievous eyes and a rather naughty little face.'

Hammond, who lived with guitarist Jeff Beck for nearly 20 years and has been a life-long campaigner for animal rights, went on: 'When you get to know him well, that mischievous streak does come out in his behaviour. But he is also very insecure and I think he's never quite got rid of that. He always needs to be bolstered.

'He treated me like a queen and I feel very bad that I wasn't nice to him. But, at the end of the day, being treated like a queen can become a bit overpowering. I had to leave New York and come back to Britain and become my own person again. But I'm still terribly fond of him. I'd like to see him happy and settled.'

Their relationship faded. Hammond returned to London and then flew back again. The separations were gnawing away at them. On that next trip to Manhattan she decided to leave him and meet up with Terence Donovan in Miami.

Celia Hammond was in Florida. Dudley was on the couch in New York and spent the next couple of decades consulting psychiatrists. Of his initial therapist he says: 'It was pretty fascinating, though very embarrassing at times. Spouting on about my hidden lusts. The trouble was I couldn't shock him. He just sat there. I felt frustrated by it all. I got very annoyed, shouting: "Why don't you bloody well say something!" All he said was: "Why does that make you annoyed."'

Psychiatrist Dr Glen Wilson claims that it is Dudley's insecurity about his height that makes him so attracted to tall women. 'It's as if he wants to prove to the world that height is no drawback when it comes to love. Most small men don't go for tall woman or vice-versa, but Dudley probably feels he's a big enough man socially to measure up to much taller women. He's making a public statement about his own self-esteem. He's saying: "Look at me, I'm enough of a man to be able to attract a woman of this stature."'

By the time *Beyond the Fringe* ended in America in 1964, lover-boy had all but forgotten Celia Hammond and was living in his smart apartment with British model Cynthia Cassidy. That ended. Dudley had yet another fancy.

He was suddenly smitten by Shirley Ann Field, who had won rave reviews opposite Albert Finney in *Saturday Night and Sunday Morning* in 1960 and had impressed critics in *The Damned* a year later. She was stunning, sexy and successful. They had a passionate but not long-lasting romance. In the Sixties people, especially Dudley, wanted to 'move on'. Any thought of settling down, of permanent, monogamous relationships, felt like a concrete overcoat. Dudley had returned to London to rent an apartment in Mayfair owned by George Hastings. These, as he said, were to be his first major sex-symbol days. Gillian Lynne recounts his anger about his club foot, saying: 'He wanted to be an Adonis. And he wasn't.

The past, as always, haunted him, as it would do all his life. For others, it never seemed to matter the way it always has for him.

One time when he was particularly depressed, and moaning and whining about his disability, Gillian Lynne repaid all the help he had given her by cradling his misshapen leg in her arms and telling him it was 'beautiful'.

Nanny knew best, especially this particular 'Mary Poppins', who understands Dudley as much as anyone. She knew how a spoonful of sugar could help the reality go down.

Dudley may not have been Adonis, but the former Sadler's Wells star said of him: 'Still the women fell like flies around him. I would have done so too, if I hadn't been working with him.'

CHAPTER FIVE

Lost and Found

'I don't know why Dudley took so long to find himself. I found him years ago.'

Peter Cook

Dudley was back in Britain and living in Mayfair's Shepherd Market — because of the graciousness of Old Etonian George Hastings — with restaurants like 'Tiddy Dolls' and glorious 'hot' pubs, and where many ladies who only spoke English gave exotic French lessons. He had the sideburns and the hair cascading over his neck that epitomised the kipper-tie times. The Beatnik era was over. These were *stylish* times. There were the Chelsea boots, flared trousers and the splashed Picasso-style shirts. Most people looked as though they had got dressed in the dark. Co-ordination in the Sixties was as much lost in the wardrobe as it was in the mind. These were the turn-on, tune-in days of American go-go guru Timothy Leary. The sermon was: Lose your mind. Escape.

But Dudley's drug was work. His other habit was the ladies.

'Dudley has a sort of magnetic attraction for girls,' his friend George Hastings, double-bass player, Norfolk landowner and barrister, would later recall. 'When he used to play with his jazz trio at the Establishment there would always be a ring of girls standing around the piano with their eyes fixed on Dudley, each one hoping he would take them home. He appeals to every instinct girls have, including the mother instinct. And I don't think he knew then just how attractive he was.'

These were not times to have a yawn. When the original *Beyond the Fringe* troop split up, three members were buying impressive properties in London (Miller and Bennett still lived in the same homes in 1995) and Dudley was leaping into expensive motor cars. Give me a Maserati! Give me a Ferrari! Curiously, his image in the mid-Sixties of the with-it swinger would mirror that of the madcap Malibu sex maniac, which would later bring him Hollywood notoriety.

At the time he just wanted to enjoy himself. If he had got rather lost in the Americas, he had found himself back in frantically changing Britain.

Champagne and lemon-flavoured ice lollies, rather than caviar, were important parts of the menu and were always in the freezer box in the boot of his screamingly upmarket cars.

Peter Cook had plunged himself into *Private Eye*. Jonathan Miller was working furiously at the Arts on television, especially British television's arts show *Monitor*. Alan Bennett, the real academic, was studying and writing. BBC2 was the 'new' channel and Dudley did some impressive turns, which involved a couple of appearances by Peter Cook on the series *Offbeat*. One sketch was the embryo of Pete 'n' Dud. It had two working-class cretins talking about their lives with the famous.

In one scene Cook is on the telephone and announces down the line: 'Goodbye for ever.' He turns around to explain: 'That was that bloody Sophia Loren again.'

Dudley loved Cook's material. It made him laugh and they could be hilariously vulgar to each other. Crabs up Raquel Welch's bottom and eating them out were favoured topics; and Mae West always wanting them to come up and see her sometime. In extraordinary places.

Dudley Moore and Peter Cook, 'Pete 'n' Dud', Derek and Clive – all their incarnations were step-laddered on their own intimate understanding of each other. They were a double act – in their particular period – on the scale of Laurel and Hardy, and Abbott and Costello. They are classics now because, like the Monty Python team and John Cleese's *Fawlty Towers*, they did not push too hard or too long. A taste in entertainment, they understood, is better than a bloating meal.

Of course, they still belched a lot. But Pete 'n' Dud were never greedy. Just desperate to get it right. To please. And to be applauded.

Peter Cook was the perfect partner for Dudley. In the last interview before his death he was asked about his happiest moments, and he talked of Dudley and their television work together: 'I don't know how long it would have gone on, but it just seemed by chance perfectly natural. I mean it was *ideal*. I can't imagine a comedy relationship being better.

'I *adore* Dudley. I would have been very happy to continue working with him. I doubt I will ever do anything better,' he said, in a self-fulfilling prophecy. They first met in an Indian restaurant in Soho, and Cook recalled: 'Dudley was very shy and quiet. I was very loud. The main thing I remember was the food. It was revolting.'

At Cambridge, Cook was expecting to join the Foreign Office, but even in the summer of 1959 there was talk of his comic genius. Impresario Michael Codron lunched with the late actor Kenneth Williams, who became so well-known through the *Carry On* films, and later Williams noted of Codron in his published diaries: 'He has found some v. good material from a boy called Peter Cook from Cambridge.'

That 'material' became the centre of the successful stage revue *Pieces of Eight*, which starred Williams and Fenella Fielding long before the 'satire boom' that resulted in David Frost's *That Was The Week That Was* and a blazing Catherine wheel of spin-offs. Harold Pinter wrote some of the sketches, which had 'poetic' pauses. Cook was upset. They were being paid on a time-scale. Although he had produced most of the material, Pinter was getting more loot. 'Talk of pay-pauses,' he complained.

But Cook was not put off. He wrote *One Over the Eight*, which was produced at the Duke of York Theatre in 1961 just as he was embarking as one of the *Beyond the Fringe* foursome.

'I was sort of blown into show business. I didn't

really have any ambitions to learn my craft as a performer. If it had involved any hard graft I'd have given up very early on. That sounds appalling, but I'd have been perfectly happy at the Foreign Office.

His father was a colonial officer in Nigeria and Peter inherited what he called 'the lordly mien of a forest *bwana*, stiff-upper-lipped at the news that the natives are growing restless'. His grandmother brought him up in Torquay – there were fears of malaria in Nigeria – and Peter Edward Cook, born on 17 November 1937, was a rebel from the start. A rebel with a seaside cause. He witnessed all that was, and is, awful about Britain, driving around his home town. Who were these people invading Torquay, buckets and spades at the ready?

At Radley and Pembroke College, Cambridge, his contemporaries included politicians of today, such as Michael Howard, Kenneth Clarke and Leon Brittan, of whom he later said: 'It's a bit distressing when you think of them running the country; they were so self-important at 20 that you would have thought they would have grown out of it.' Cook read modern languages and planned on joining the Diplomatic Corps. It ran in the family.

But his pen ran away with his thoughts. He wrote 'Black and White Blues' about a Salvation Army band with a jazz beat, which went to Africa to convert the natives. 'It was diabolical but people still come up to me and say: "That thing you did at Radley was the best bloody thing you ever did. You've gone off since then."'

But he liked his university lifestyle: 'I had a life of complete luxury in my last year. I don't think I've ever laughed so much. I was already at Cambridge. I had two fags. I had breakfast in bed. I used to go to the pictures and fish for trout in a lake. I did a bit of teaching, a bit of lying in fields. And I organised bootleg games of soccer, because football wasn't allowed. It was delightful.'

Dudley missed National Service because of his leg, Cook because of feathers. 'You may laugh, but it's serious. They asked me if I was put in a barrack room with feather pillows would I keep sneezing, and in all honesty I had to say yes. I'm not sure whether the allergy was brought on by carrying a white feather with me wherever I went.'

He went to Europe. He returned to Britain. He tried to drop his plummy upper-class accent while Dudley was trying to soften his Essex vowels.

On his death, Cook was hailed as the 'father' of modern satire. As a man who could just do it. It was in him. 'He was the greatest creator of comic material I have ever come across,' said John Cleese, who in Cook's later years became a close friend.

The tall *Monty Python* man, known around the world for this madcap series and for ever as Basil in *Fawlty Towers*, went on: 'It was always discouraging. Whereas most of us would take six hours to write a good three-minute sketch, it actually took Peter three minutes. I always thought he was the best of us and the only one who came near being a genius, because genius, to me, has something to do with doing it much more easily than other people.'

Cook was called 'probably the funniest Englishman since Chaplin' by the broadcaster David Dimbleby and, when confronted with the comment, he replied: 'Well, this is no time for false modesty.'

He reinvented British satire. He became Lord Gnome at *Private Eye* and was proud of his 'very good bad taste', but he left it to the editors, first Richard Ingrams and later Ian Hislop, to make the decisions.

In the 'You've never had it so good' days of Harold 'Supermac' Macmillan, the *Beyond the Fringe* crowd's only direct political spoof was a take-off of the Prime Minister. Cook did the crowingly complacent imitation of Macmillan.

'The idea that Cook had an anarchic, subversive view of society is complete nonsense,' says Jonathan Miller, adding: 'He was the most upstanding, traditional upholder of everything English and everything establishment.'

Alan Bennett agrees: 'He wasn't interested in satire at all. He was interested in being funny. I think he didn't like some of the harder-edged stuff because it wasn't funny enough. He wasn't particularly into making points.

'The thing that was political was his imitation of Macmillan. Nobody had ever done that on-stage before. When Macmillan came to the show, everybody in the audience knew he was there, so it was quite funny to begin with. But then Peter just started going for him, and he went on and on, until the audience fell nearly totally silent. It never bothered him if he lost the audience. He was immune to embarrassment.'

The Establishment Club, which took over what was formerly a strip club – a fact that titillated the new owner – was Cook's power base. It has been likened to the pre-World War Two 'Cabaret' rooms of Berlin. The unique, controversial and clever but heroin-addicted American entertainer Lenny Bruce made his British début there. 'Lenny Bruce was a revelation,' said Cook, continuing: 'I watched him every night for four weeks and I never got over it. He was never allowed back into Britain after that visit. The last I heard of him before his death was that he'd jumped from the window of his apartment in America crying "I am SUPERJEW" and broken both his ankles. But never was a "serious" comedian so misunderstood or so maliciously maligned.'

Bruce was performing at the Establishment one evening when Irish actress Siobhan McKenna marched out in anger. She had a 'fight' with Cook, who charged her with scratching his face. 'These hands are clean. These are Irish hands and they are clean.' It was that time in the evening. Cook didn't miss a beat and replied: 'Well, this is a British face and it's bleeding.'

Cambridge contemporaries like John Bird and Eleanor Bron also performed there. Barry Humphries, whom Cook encouraged and helped – Humphries wrote the words for *Private Eye*'s classic 'Barry MacKenzie' comic strip – débuted Dame Edna Everage at the Establishment.

'Peter's generosity was unusual in a profession notoriously self-seeking and fraught with petty jealousies,' says Humphries, who would sit in the club thinking, creating and tapping his feet to the man at the piano – Dudley Moore.

Pete 'n' Dud. The tall Cook, the diminutive Moore, a visual laugh before a word was spoken. 'Magisterial in their mischief,' said the critics. John Bird calls it 'a spontaneous combustion of comic invention'.

Cook's friend Martin Lewis, who produced 1982's *The Secret Policemen's Other Ball* recalls that Cook wanted the movie *Bedazzled* to be titled *Raquel Welch*.

'Why?' asked Lewis.

'I'd like the marquee to read "Peter Cook and Dudley Moore in Raquel Welch",' explained Cook, who added sadly: 'For some reason the distributors don't see the point.'

Many people didn't. Cook, like Dudley, used humour to guard against his enemies. 'I suppose I have some regrets but I can't remember what they are,' he said, trying to fob off questions about why he had not become a superstar. Sometimes, but only sometimes, he would get irritated and shoot off 'I don't give a toss if people say I haven't fulfilled my promise.' He would glory in his indolent lifestyle: 'I think I ran out of ambition at 24. If the weather isn't fine I'll spend a lot of the week reading the newspapers or watching Brazilian soap operas. Life is a matter of passing the time enjoyably.'

Humour, as always, was the shield, but his friends rather than his cohorts sense a sadness about Peter

Cook that was more evident in the later years, when he knew the drinking, smoking and carousing had taken their toll on his body. He was, of course, clever enough to know what was going on. It didn't stop him joking. Or drinking.

But long before his death he was upset by his 'divorce' from Dudley. Of Dudley's success in America he would say: 'I'm glad it hasn't changed him. He's still selfish, vain, greedy. In other words, a fully rounded human being.' Barry Humphries comments: 'Peter had too much of a sense of the cosmic joke to ever reveal self-pity. I got the feeling of sorrow – sorrow about the end of the Dudley Moore alliance. Peter felt enormous frustration. I think rage is not an exaggeration.'

It was 1977 when Pete 'n' Dud broke up professionally. They never did emotionally. It was one of those relationships that naturally beat the time, the years or the place: just by a meeting or a phone call. 'You little, fucking club-footed cunt' would be offered like a hand in friendship. When Dudley soared off to superstardom, Alan Bennett says: 'Greatly to his credit, Peter didn't resent the fact that Dudley had taken off. Dudley can't write. Peter could and all the sketches were written by Peter. And then Dudley took off and made a fortune in Hollywood.'

In his down moments Dudley has always admitted to a 'disease' that lay between him and Cook in the 15 or so years before Cook's death.

Previously their relationship had been infectious. For millions of people. But for no one more than Dudley.

Cook had married three times and had adoring daughters, Lucy and Daisy, from his Cambridge love and first wife Wendy Snowden, whom he married in 1963. They lived in H.G. Wells's former home in Hampstead. It had William Morris wallpaper, Tiffany lamps and the aspiring, benevolent upper-middle class look that Cook and his followers would so wonderfully send up. In 1971 this picture-framed life ended. In 1973 Cook married actress Judy Huxtable, whom he nicknamed 'Sexburga'. They separated five years later.

He had known Malaysian-Chinese property dealer Lin Chong for seven years before they married in 1989. Even then they continued to live in different houses – one hundred yards apart. As always, Cook needed 'space'. On his death, she was the main beneficiary of his estate, which included a 40 per cent sharehold in *Private Eye* – the 'organ', as Cook called it – worth about £1 million. Cook's younger sisters, Sarah and Elizabeth, received the remaining 16 per cent of his majority *Eye* holdings.

On the day of Cook's death, Dudley, who clearly could not comprehend the loss of his partner, reacted this way: 'Peter was selfish and I admired that. He was a thoroughly hedonistic guy. But it wasn't selfishness in the way we all think of that word. It was selfishness because he did what he wanted. He was happy appearing on Hampstead High Street in slippers to get the papers in the morning. He didn't mind how he was interpreted. Peter hadn't been well and his wife Lin called to tell me he had been taken to hospital for an operation on his liver. I had grave feelings about that.

'I felt rather numb, which I suppose is the only way to describe it. And yet, despite the shock, I can't say it's a big surprise. I thought this might happen at some point.

'I last saw him in England in 1994. I called him later, around Easter, and we always stayed in touch on the phone. I'd call him when I was depressed about things. He wanted me to come back in 1995 and do some revue material with him. I think he was quite keen but I didn't want to do that.

'I would never have made it without Peter. He was the creative genius, the driving force behind our partnership. He had 17 ideas to one of mine. Mine were very suburban and tame, but his were always extraordinary flights of fancy. If he had a fault, it was that Pete was relentless in making everyone laugh. He had a verbal wit that was second to none, but sometimes he overdid it.

'I remember him at parties that we used to have after recordings of our TV show and he made sure people were laughing. That was one of his qualities. But he kept on bludgeoning people with his wit.

'There was a certain relentless quality to him, which was not a good thing. But he could always make me laugh and made me look funny. Alan Bennett has said that together Pete and I were tremendously funny in *Beyond the Fringe*, but if a joke was funny it would be Pete's. I couldn't contribute a damned thing except for the musical skits and a couple of lines. Pete was always producing a barrage of great wit. And it's thanks to Pete that he let me have my neck and go further, because I was restless after *Beyond the Fringe*, where I just did musical parodies.

'We came together at a time when we were both very ambitious and loved what we were doing. But Pete with his great intellect was able to talk about anything, and so Dud 'n' Pete – the two Cockney characters – were allowed to take on such massive subjects as religion and sex, on which we could pompously pontificate – things that we had no idea about. Pete was the real know-it-all just like his character. He did know about almost everything.

'He wasn't in the habit of regaling you with his knowledge but there were times when you couldn't understand some of the things he said.

'But you could always understand his jokes and he was very generous in sharing them around. Pete was very prolific and really didn't mind about the ownership of it, or who said the line, but I came up with so few lines that the one time I invented one he said: "Son of a gun!" It was a sketch set in Heaven and Pete said: "Bloody hell, we're in Heaven." He could write the funniest jokes.

'He lived a very full life. He ate too much, drank too much, smoked too much and did everything else too much. I tend to be more conservative. But it meant that he had a great, extraordinary life.'

That other legendary laughter-maker Eric Sykes rather summed up the crucial differences between the two friends and partners: 'Of course, Dudley Moore has done very well and Peter didn't. But I think that was because he was not prepared to do what other people wanted. He wanted to do what he wanted.'

With Cook's death, Dudley had lost a friend, a prop and a witty pen. But the memories are still there. The two of them brought lunatic fun to television in 1965 with *Not Only . . . But Also* (NOBA). It was landmark material. John Lennon wanted to appear and did. Dudley's idol Peter Sellers asked to be on the show. He was.

The series ran for four years on BBC2. Dud 'n' Pete would sit in their matching cloth caps and scarves, eating turned-up sandwiches and philosophising about the meaning of life and art. They would dream exotic fantasies in which they were plagued by Hollywood sex symbols. 'That Rita Hayworth was all over me but I wasn't having any!'

They had sharp-edged humour, and Dudley learned from every moment he spent with Cook. His partner's extemporising often had Dudley convulsed with giggles. They had one sketch set in an art gallery, with Cook explaining to Dud how bottoms follow you around the room. As ignoramuses Pete 'n' Dud, their contribution was surreal.

Dud: 'Did I tell you about that girl Joan Harold who I used to know? She used to travel on the 148 bus route a lot. At 6 p.m. every evening she used to get the 148 bus home. I used to leave work about 5 p.m., as you know, about ten miles from where she was but I always felt I had to see her, so what I used to do, I used to come out of work, I used to get the 62B up to Chadwell Heath Merry Fiddlers, then I used to go down the hill and get the 514 trolley down to Rainham Crescent. Then I used to go over by the railway bridge and go across those fields by the dye works . . . I'd come out the other side by the hedge by which time the 148 bus, the six o' clock one, was coming round the corner, Hobbs Hill. Now, it used to come round very slowly, 'cos it was a very sharp turn, and there's no bus stop there but it used to be very slow. If it was going too fast I used to lay down in the middle of the road, but what I used to do, I used to leap on the platform as it went past 'cos I knew she was on that bus.'

Pete: 'What happened then, Dud?'

Dud: 'Well, I used to lay panting on the platform for about ten minutes.'

And then there were was the legend of 'One Leg Too Few'.

Cook, as a theatrical producer, is auditioning Dudley as Mr Spiggott ('Spiggott by name, Spiggott by nature') for the role of Tarzan. Dudley has one leg. Cook says: 'I couldn't help noticing almost at once that you are a one-legged person. You, a lone-legged person, are applying for the role of Tarzan, a role which traditionally involves the use of a two-legged actor.'

It went on:

Cook: 'Need I point out to you where the deficiency lies as regards landing this role?'

Dudley: 'Yes, I think you ought to.'

Cook: 'Need I say with over-much emphasis that it is in the leg division that you are deficient.'

Dudley: 'The leg division?'

Cook: 'Yes, the leg division, Mr Spiggott. You are deficient in it to the tune of one. Your right leg I like. I like your right leg. A lovely leg for the role. That's what I said when I saw it come in. I said: "A lovely leg for the role." I've nothing against your right leg. The trouble is – neither have you.'

Watched again in 1995, the sketch still works and Dudley was especially good. His character is so convinced he would make an excellent Tarzan that the idea runs riot around itself as he hops about as the would-be Johnny Weissmuller. But it's wonderfully 'Me Tarzan, you Pete.'

'I've got nothing against your right leg' became a British pub phrase for years. Especially in the men's lavatory not long before closing time.

The 45-minute bi-weekly series of *Not Only . . . But Also* began on 9 January 1965, and there were two more series – weekly half-hours – one a year later and the next in 1970. Cook's creation E.L. Wisty – the park-bench flat-voiced droning monologue moron merchant – and the Pete 'n' Dud performances were helped along by Dudley's musical trio and guest artists. But Pete 'n' Dud were the certified stars, signing off with 'Goodbye-ee!'

'Goodbye-ee' went into the British music charts when they released it as a single. As did Cook's 'The Ballad of Spotty Muldoon' with Dudley playing violin and piano. This terrific twosome were the toast of the town.

Someone said around this time that satirists, like spiders, always end up devouring each other. But Pete 'n' Dud were an exception. They thrived on each other, although even with all the success, Dudley would tire of the Pete 'n' Dud act.

'I found that I got exhausted every time we did these sketches. It didn't matter who we were – Laurel and Hardy or whoever – you had to work at keeping the pace and the energy up.

'To even things up we would have a go at other things. One of my favourites was a spoof of Tom Jones. I played him singing "It's Not Unusual" with a Beethoven-German accent. Peter was Francisco José de Goya, the celebrated Spanish artist. It was great fun.

'Everything with Peter was great fun.'

As was Dudley's life.

CHAPTER SIX

Suzy and the Movies

'He hasn't changed over the years I've known him.'

Dudley's first wife, Suzy Kendall

As supercharged as his cars, the young, successful, swinging Dudley Moore drove around London in a black Maserati Mistrale. Drinks in the Chelsea Potter on the King's Road, cocktails at the West End spots and in Soho, which by now was a home from home. Greek Street was as familiar as the piano. It seemed he could have any 'dolly bird' he wanted. He wanted Suzy Kendall. She was a 'Darling', like Julie Christie, with the essential 'uniform' of the day: big smile and big, cascading blonde curls, and generous in other areas that Dudley likes, too. And 5ft 4in tall. Born in 1944, she was nine years younger than Dudley.

He was overwhelmed by her. Smitten. Lustful. In love. All of it. Dudley wrote love letters. And notes. He was besotted.

But he wanted Suzy Kendall to be just for him. He didn't want to share her with the outside world. Previously he had happily flaunted his relationships, but this time it was for *him*.

The hair, the teeth and the smile were real but Suzy

Kendall, actress and model, was in reality Frieda Harriet Harrison, born and brought up a convent girl in Belper, Derbyshire. Like Dudley, her roots were working-class. Her father was a builder and decorator. They had both moved on. She was a graduate of Derby Art College who had moved down to London and, ironically, had got involved in marriage to a jazz musician, Jeff Arnold, that lasted just six months.

She, like Dudley, was very much part of London's Swinging Sixties, with her flat in Elystan Place off Chelsea's King's Road. Most of the major and ground-breaking talent of the times either lived or spent most of their time in Chelsea. It was 'the scene' for the second half of the Sixties.

Mary Quant was getting her husband to cut her pubic hair into heart shapes and Chelsea Football Club was the team to follow. Dick Lester was directing *A Hard Day's Night* and *Help!* with the Beatles and the later-to-be-idolised John Boorman was working with the Dave Clark Five in *Catch Us If You Can*. Sean Connery as James Bond was making vodka martinis and Balkan Sobranie cigarettes popular. Then came Michael Caine in the movie adaptation of Len Deighton's *The Ipcress File*. Tony Richardson – then married to Vanessa Redgrave – was a barrier-breaking director, much as his associate John Osborne was as a writer.

Kitchen-sink drama had been established but by then washed down the drain. The Oxbridge boys were the new players on the cutting-edge. It was a sharp place to be.

In 1965 in the middle of that epoch-making decade Dudley and Peter Cook made their celluloid bow in *The Wrong Box*. It was, as it turned out, the wrong movie. But then it was trumpet time. And for obvious reasons. The cast list ran like the credits of scores of British classics: Ralph Richardson, John Mills, Peter Sellers, Michael Caine, Cicely Courtneidge, Irene Handl, Wilfrid Lawson, Nanette Newman (Mrs Bryan Forbes) and, historically, the great wonder of the comic world, Tony Hancock, who took his own life in 1968. Pete 'n' Dud and Sellers and Hancock together in one film takes the breath away. Sadly, none of them had the hindsight to realise what an event it was.

Equally sadly, the movie directed by Bryan Forbes was a Carnaby Street meets Robert Louis Stevenson mishap rather than a masterpiece. 'I never found what Bryan did very easy to follow,' said Dudley, adding: 'I disagreed with Bryan a great deal about his approach to comedy. It was like aping movements and facial expressions, even though it wasn't constantly like that. He gave you very little room to do your own thing. I like him very much, so it wasn't all that negative. I've seen the film a few times and I've never been able to quite understand what goes on in it – probably because I was so obsessed with the discomfort I went through when I did the film.'

With Suzy Kendall it was different. He was doing *their* thing.

Dudley's great love for Suzy Kendall at that time did not threaten the independence of either of them. She was her own woman with a yellow E-type Jaguar and credits in movies like *Circus of Fear* and *To Sir With Love* – title song by Lulu – co-starring Sidney Poitier. By then they were living together.

Their live-in relationship had been speeded along by a break-in at Suzy's apartment. She and Dudley had walked in while the thieves were still there. There was jostling and shoving, but nothing more serious than Suzy's television being rushed out the door by the robbers. Nevertheless, it prompted this new 'swinging' couple to look for a home of their own.

They found it in Hampstead. A house on a hill, the Mount in Heath Street, which was everything they aspired to: it was old (Georgian) and secluded (with a walled garden), and it had what neither of them had ever had growing up: it had room. Seven bedrooms, an underground running stream, and the rest.

For Dudley this was love and fun in overload. How could life be better? A Hampstead haven, a Maserati and an exquisite lady.

Enter a Hollywood offer.

Not Only . . . But Also directed by Joe McGarth was on television, *The Wrong Box* had opened in cinemas, and 20th Century Fox wanted Stanley Donen – the Stanley Donen of *Singin' in the Rain*, *Funny Face*, *Seven Brides for Seven Brothers* – to direct Pete 'n' Dud in a movie.

The boys had the idea for *Bedazzled* and Peter Cook wrote the script. Dudley composed the music. Raquel Welch provided other parts. Essential ones. Dudley was his old friend Stanley Moon.

Stanley is a Wimpy bar chef and Peter Cook is the Devil, aka Mr Spiggott. It's a Faustian relationship.

Stanley enquires of Spiggott how his career began.

Spiggott: 'It was pride that got me into this.'

Stanley: 'Oh, yes, you used to be God's favourite, didn't you?'

Spiggott: 'That's right. "I Love Lucifer" it used to be in those days.'

Stanley Moon is a bundle of self-début doubts, just as Dudley was in those early days. They were both plump psychiatrist couch-potatoes. Stanley doesn't know who he is. It's not just spots and his height and his sex life, it's *everything*. Later, Peter Cook would explain that his *Bedazzled* creation was really an exaggeration of his partner. Cook saw more than he ever allowed and he never, ever used his incredible insight to upset or manipulate Dudley. The dagger of his wit was aimed at others. Dudley, if anything, got the occasional nick. His blood was almost always spared.

It was all Heaven for Dudley – he thought he'd made a deal with the Devil in real life. Suzy Kendall was loving and adoring, and they created the epitome of the Sixties' lifestyle for themselves. The invitations to dinner, to openings and to every 'happening' crowded their letter box. Hot? They were Barbados in July. At home Dudley had all the sex he wanted. At the movies he had Raquel Welch, as Lillian Lust, pressing his fresh face into her bulging black-bra-levered bosom.

Many people wanted to be Stanley Moon. And Dudley Moore. Preferably both.

The critics were not dazzled by *Bedazzled*, but it did all right and certainly did nothing to diminish the cult of Pete 'n' Dud.

When it was released Dudley was living in Chelsea with Suzy Kendall. 'Dudley moved in with me about four months after we met. I had been living with a girl-friend and we lived in that apartment for about a year and half after she moved out. That was before we bought the house in Hampstead.

'It was wild there. We had five Persian cats – Charlie, Sadie (after Sadie Thompson), Ada (after Dudley's mother) and two others that we just called "Cats". We were inseparable then. I couldn't stand being apart from him for a day, never mind a week, which his work – or mine – sometimes meant. When he was at home we would play ping-pong [table-tennis] or just relax. We loved to relax and be together.

'Dudley loved to go out driving. He had these "hot" cars. And I loved my E-type. It wasn't showing off. It was making use of what we had. We adored each other and we still do. It's just one of these things. I don't think many of these really passionate relationships of the Sixties were ever going to last. But luckily our friendship has lasted over all the years.'

It may be his Dagenham frugality, but Dudley still stays with his first wife on some trips to London. She has remarried twice and still lives in the home that she and Dudley bought three decades ago.

In 1968 she appeared in the then notable film *Up the Junction* as the middle-class girl who goes to live on the wrong side of the tracks in London's Clapham. The same year it was *30 Is a Dangerous Age, Cynthia* and marriage to Dudley, whose frustration with the flop of *Bedazzled* was beginning to show. He decided to do something without Peter Cook, and *Cynthia* – there is no such character but it came from his affair with Cynthia Cassidy – was it. He wrote the screenplay and it was blatantly and often embarrassingly autobiographical. John Wells and Joe McGarth (who also directed) joined up to help with the screenplay.

Dudley played the obscure musician Rupert Street who, at 29, feels his life vanishing. He wants to be a success before he reaches 30. The film is packed with real-life links, including Suzy Kendall's character, who comes from Derbyshire; and 'Rupert Street' is actually a Soho thoroughfare. Dudley says that his mother should have got a credit: 'She always sent me my laundry through the mail – just like Rupert's mother in the film. And just like Rupert's mother, she always included a sack of lemon drops and some bread puddings in the package.'

'Dudley has got a very happy way of inventing dialogue and is certainly one of the funniest of men in private life. However, there was a stage when he was first going through analysis that he thought he had to be deadly serious,' said John Wells. 'Once during shooting he sat in the middle of a group of cameramen telling them that the reason he had trouble producing scripts was because of potty training.

'Nobody laughed at all, as it was done with the

utmost seriousness. I think that's what Peter teased him about most and what Jonathan and Alan thought about him – that he gets too easily drawn into being profound. Whereas his great gift is not to be profound – his gift is being a fantastic clown.'

Dudley clowned in *Cynthia* along with the Johns – Bird and Wells – and Patricia Routledge, who in the 1990s was to find greater fame in Britain as the star of the television series *Keeping Up Appearances*, Hyacinth 'Bouquet' Bucket. But *Cynthia* wasn't dangerous. It was dull.

Dudley's marriage wasn't much of an event either.

He married Frieda Harriet Harrison at Hampstead Register Office on 14 June 1968. It was all kept secret. Peter Cook knew about it, but it was very low-key. Cook and Eastender Pat Booth, by the 1990s a best-selling novelist based in Palm Beach, Florida, were the witnesses. 'I had no idea they were getting married until Suzy phoned me to say that it had happened,' said Dudley's secretary Diana Borghys.

After the ceremony there were belated 'happy snaps' for the newspaper photographers, but after marriage their lives returned to what they had been before. They had 'the bit of paper' but that was the only difference.

Except that Dudley was restless.

Professionally, he was at a crossroads. The Seventies loomed. He and Peter Cook did their usual double act in *Those Daring Young Men in their Jaunty Jalopies* (also known as *Monte Carlo or Bust*), but it was a wander through the park for them. Their co-stars included

Tony Curtis and Dudley's hero Terry Thomas. Nothing helped. The film, which was dreamed up as a hilarious follow-up to *Those Magnificent Men in Their Flying Machines*, crash-landed at the box office. In one of those it's-a-small-world ironies, Blake Edwards had re-started this epic comic-caper movie genre in 1965 with Curtis, Jack Lemmon and Natalie Wood in the classic *The Great Race*.

But Dudley wasn't finding any classics at the end of the Sixties. He and Cook were cast in *The Bed-Sitting Room*, which had been written by John Antrobus and another of Dudley's idols, Spike Milligan. It was a hap-penstance project resulting from the death of playwright Joe Orton in August 1967, which left direc-tor Richard Lester with a budget but no screenplay. Lester had a deal with Columbia Pictures to do a musi-cal involving Mick Jagger, but instead ended up filming the surreal apocalyptic play, which was always a the-atrical project. For many it is now a fond memory because of the cast, which included Arthur Lowe, Ralph Richardson, Marty Feldman, Dandy Nichols, Mona Washbourne, Harry Secombe – Dudley *did* get to work with his beloved Goons, but he was not enchanted by Dick Lester: 'He gave peculiar instruc-tions which were hard to follow. He's a very nice man, cheerful and affable, but there was nothing you could do to please him. He wanted different opinions but rejected them all, which was very disconcerting.'

Dudley, as always, detested rejection, which was what *The Bed-Sitting Room* got. This did not help his domestic situation. Suzy Kendall was doing well in film, working for Hollywood producers in movies like *Darker than Amber* and Italy's *The Bird with a Crystal Plumage*. You only have to be with Dudley for moments to know that what matters is what is happening to *him*.

Pete 'n' Dud did some television work together in America and Britain, including a show in which their guest was Anne Bancroft, the wife of Mel Brooks. She was then a sensation as Mrs Robinson, the lust of Dustin Hoffman in his breakthrough film *The Graduate* and immortalised in song by Simon and Garfunkel. Not surprisingly, Peter Cook wrote a parody of *The Graduate* for her.

But Dudley was drifting apart from Cook. And from Suzy Kendall. Entertainment engineer and jack-of-all-jokes-and-shows Barry Took was working for the BBC's comedy division in 1971. One of his shows as a producer involved Sheila Hancock, later to become Mrs John 'Inspector Morse' Thaw. It had the delightfully daffy actress singing, dancing and chatting with the, hopefully, appropriate guest star. *But Seriously – It's Sheila Hancock* was to be amusing, but only in sequences.

For one such 'take' Barry Took employed the services of Dudley Moore. It was to be a play on the film version of *Brief Encounter* with Dudley in Trevor Howard's role as the doctor and Sheila Hancock filling Celia Johnson's shoes as the confused married woman. The idea was that Hancock is a singer whose husband will only allow her to sing melody, while Dudley's wife will only let him sing harmony. They meet in the railway station cafeteria. He whistles a tune. She hums another. They talk and fall in love. Harmony and melody for ever?

It was not to be. Took says: 'The buffet set was a perfect replica of the one in *Brief Encounter* where Trevor Howard and Celia Johnson had their emotional meetings, and the costumes were to be the same Forties period. All went well at rehearsals; however, when it came to the recording Sheila looked fine in her tailored suits but Dudley in a double-breasted fawn raincoat and trilby hat looked faintly ridiculous . . . No – come to think of it – he looked ludicrous. They started the sketch and after a few lines Sheila giggled. They started again and Dudley giggled. At the third attempt they both giggled, and after that for at least four more takes one or other would break down in tears of unsuppressible mirth.

'By now the studio audience were screaming with uncontrollable laughter and I decided that, as clearly the sketch was never going to emerge coherently, we might as well abandon it and go on with the next item.

'Dudley did his best but he looked so funny in the Forties hat and coat meant for someone of Trevor Howard's stature, and with his innocent face belied by twinkling eyes suggesting a whole work of mischief, we could never have completed the sketch. And if you don't believe me, try whistling while you're laughing.'

Dud 'n' Pete, Pete 'n' Dud, and what of Dud and Suzy?

Cook went off to work with David Frost on the film

The Rise and Rise of Michael Rimmer. The grand American theatrical producer David Merrick invited Dudley to take the lead in a London West End run of Woody Allen's *Play it Again, Sam*. The play – and later the film with Allen and his muse Diane Keaton – is all about a little guy's attempts to get laid. In doing so, he calls up the spirit of Humphrey Bogart. It's all absurd and silly, and tremendously entertaining.

And Dudley did well with Allen's material. Woody Allen – he and Dudley are the same age, transatlantic performing 'cousins' – was, and is, a master of neurotic behaviour. Dudley was the perfect jockey for such material. He rewrote Allen to give the show more of a British 'ear'.

On-stage Dudley was playing the part. At home he was living it. Both he and Suzy Kendall were regularly on the psychiatrist's couch.

As any good psychiatrist could have told them, their marriage was not going to work. She felt 'lost' and didn't want to be 'a Dudley Moore appendage', and he became increasingly frustrated. And prone to long silences. He would brood, go back to his university days' habit of skulking in corners. He was not happy.

'With Suzy I was very repressed, very contained in myself, but I knew that she knew all that was going on inside me and didn't have to comment on it. She, in a sense, let me be. She believed in her own feelings, which was only something I was just learning to do, to believe in *my own* feelings.'

As the Seventies began, Dudley moved in with his

trusted and long-time supporter George Hastings, taking the ground floor of George and his wife Alys's house in London's Camden Town.

On 15 September 1972, two years after they separated, Dudley and Suzy's divorce was finalised in a five-minute hearing in court in Kingston, Surrey, on the grounds of 'irretrievable breakdown'. 'I give myself a D-minus as a wife,' said Suzy. 'I'm much better as a lover. I was never able to feel like a wife. When they'd say "Mrs Moore" I always wondered who they were talking about.'

Dudley, naturally, confessed later that he could not express his feelings to his wife; instead he would go into his long, unsettling silences. He was 'difficult' to live with.

He had lost a spouse, but had found his partner again and reunited with Peter Cook. They starred in *Behind the Fridge*, which had been inspired by their days in New York with *Beyond the Fringe*. The doorman of New York's 'Barbetta' restaurant deli kept raving about their show, but with his accent it always came out as 'Behind the Fridge'. It sparked off a run in Australia, ran at the Cambridge Theatre in London and subsequently, entitled *Good Evening*, had a long run in New York before going on tour in America, where the show won the theatrical 'Oscar', a Tony Award, in 1974.

Pete 'n' Dud were stars on the gravy train. They took *Behind the Fridge* to Australia and New Zealand, and Dudley had a great time. The pressures were off and so far from home – both from London and New York – he could do his own thing: 'I couldn't think of anything more enjoyable. It was such tremendous fun and you came off-stage absolutely ecstatic and jumping about the place.'

Dudley was happy because no one was asking him for anything. Back home he had commitments to family and friends. People wanted favours. Could he appear here or play there? For this or that charity, or friend of a friend? Down Under all he had to deal with was Peter Cook, and by then that was a doddle.

While the show ran and ran around the world before opening in November 1972 in London – a show that incorporated the work of two likely lads, the now royal-approved Andrew Lloyd Webber and Tim Rice – Dudley appeared as 'The Dormouse' in a live-action film of *Alice's Adventures in Wonderland*. It was hardly a week's work, for he appears only at the Mad Hatter's Tea Party. But it reunited him with colleagues Roy Kinnear (the Cheshire Cat), Ralph Richardson (Caterpillar) and Spike Milligan (Gryphon). It also allowed him to spend time with Peter Sellers (the March Hare), whom he had rather 'missed' because of scene-scheduling on *The Wrong Box*.

The 1990s' cleavage-conscious Fiona Fullerton was the young 'Alice', but the film made less of an impression than Dudley did on the 15-year-old Fullerton. She found him 'cute and helpful'. It is not recorded what the Queen thought of the movie, which she attended at a royal performance in December 1972.

If there's jet-lag, there is also divorce-lag and Dudley

Schoolboy Dud

Choirboy Dud

Below: Beyond The Fringe. Clockwise: Dudley, Jonathan Miller, Peter Cook, Alan Bennett
(Camera Press Ltd)

Marriage number one
to Suzy Kendall
(Hulton Deutsch)

Above Lots of stars including John Mills
and Michael Caine find themselves in
'the wrong box' with Pete 'n' Dud
(The Movie Store Collection)

Dudley's Stanley Moon listens in on
the messages from Raquel Welch's
Lust
(Popperfoto)

Dudley's baby. Dud and Suzy Kendall
at the première of Rosemary's Baby
as the decade faded in 1969
(Hulton Deutsch)

Dud and Liza
(got to kill
some of her)
(Range/Bettman/UPI)

Young
marrieds.
Dud and Suzy
and 'best girl'
Pat Booth
after his first
wedding in
1968
(Hulton Deutsch)

Love me tender:
Dudley and Tuesday Weld
(Hulton Deutsch)

Oh, dear: Pete 'n' Dud
flopped as
Holmes and Watson
(The Movie Store Collection)

Left Gotcha: Dudley's 1994 Oscar night mug shot *(Popperfoto)*

Below Dud and Pete 'testing' synthetic tobacco in 1973 *(Hulton Deutsch)*

*Left
See no evil...
Dudley and
Susan Anton
before the
Monkey
French
killed their
relationship
(Hulton Deutsch)*

love you; wedding number 4 on the beach and aftermath with fourth wife
Nicole Rothschild *(Popperfoto)*

Dudley's mantra: play it again and again and again... *(Hulton Deutsch)*

Don't tie me down: Dudley and Liza on the *Arthur* set *(Range/Bettman/UPI)*

Dudley and third wife
Brogan Lane as he gets
his star on the
Hollywood Walk of
Fame in 1987
(Range / Bettman / UPI)

Below Yes, I'll make
Arthur 2. Moore and
Minelli reunited for
the sequel
(© 1988 Warner Bros Inc)

Dudley and Bo *10*
Derek
(The Kobal Collection)

Below Bachelor boy
days in Marina-Del
Rey *(© Alpha)*

Above I want to be taken seriously: Carnegie Hall *(Emma)*

Right Fourth wedding antics *(© Alpha)*

Below Punch the pixie in *Santa Claus The Movie (The Movie Store Collection)*

Above 'I'm getting married in the morning' fantasy scene for Dudley: *30 is a Dangerous Age, Cyr...* *(Hulton Deutsch)*

Left Dudley returns in 1995 to the house where he lived and the church where he played as a youngster in Dagenham, Essex

Bunny boys: Pete 'n' Dud in January 1995,
not many weeks before Cook's death *(Popperfoto)*

Right Dudley and Brogan Lane waltz into Heathrow
(© Alpha)

Left Dudley spots *Ten*

Below Proud dad Dud and his baby son in 1995

Together again:
Pete 'n' Dud in 1995
(© Alpha)

Dudley at Peter Cook's
memorial service in St. John's
Wood, May 1995
(All Action)

was a dormouse in the doldrums. But there were still sexual escapades. Three ladies who in the 1990s are now quite respectfully married had what they call 'outings' with Dudley, and one of them had a long-term off-and-on-off affair and says: 'It was completely and utterly sexual. It was fucking and fun. Neither of us had any thought of putting pressure on the other one about living together or, God forbid, marriage and that, of course, made the fucking more fun.'

But, publicly, Dudley was not broadcasting his conquest. He has always been discreet about his romances – unless to make a point.

But he *loved* the spotlight. He was the 'surprise' guest of a *This Is Your Life* in 1973 and happily trooped through another show a decade later. The first was important because his mother was still alive, but Thames Television, who produced the then Eamonn Andrews-presented tributes, have inadvertently 'wiped' the recording, so no copy exists. The same scenario is reflected in 'lost' Pete 'n' Dud shows, as well as those of so many of the classic television comics including *Hancocks* and *Steptoe and Son*.

But Dudley was still after his 'porridge' – his Chinese food and sex.

Then, he met a tall, blonde former acquaintance, who had memorably warmed his bed . . .

CHAPTER SEVEN

Tuesday

'She seduced me after she spotted me fucking the piano.'

Dudley Moore on his second wife,
Tuesday Weld

For the James Dean generation – those who grew up watching movies that starred names like Natalie Wood and Sal Mineo, and Nick Adams and Dennis Hopper – Tuesday Weld was the great female rebel. The Hollywood gossip columnists called her 'Tuesday Wild', and years later she admits she did everything to live up to their image of her as a brazen bra-brat, all cleavage and pouts and pointed attitude. It got attention. More importantly, for her family, it got work.

She was still working in 1993, playing retiring cop Robert Duvall's distraught wife as he hunts down a mentally amuck Los Angeles office worker (played by Michael Douglas), who is rampaging through the city with a temper tantrum and a seemingly endless supply of guns and ammunition.

She didn't look like the 'Tuesday Weld' who had been the delectable, but usually dangerously provocative, youngster in films like *Return to Peyton Place* (1961) and *Pretty Poison* (1968) and the temptress of Gregory Peck in *I Walk The Line* (1971). The years were on display. She had offered an admirable performance opposite Nick Nolte in an adaptation of the great American novelist Robert Stone's Vietnam novel *Dog Soldiers* which was retitled *Who'll Stop the Rain* by Hollywood in 1978. She had played a 'lost soul'.

Tuesday Weld was somewhat typecast in the role.

Susan ker Weld had prominent teeth and the same sort of outlook on life. She'd bite before being bitten.

In 1963 the 20-year-old had gone to see *Beyond the Fringe* in New York and had taken a fancy to Dudley. Before he knew it she was backstage and had him in a hired limousine with a glass of champagne in his hand and his pants down. It was a triumph for one of the leading ladies of 1957's Hollywood movie *Rally Round the Flag, Boys*, in which she was a tempting babysitter for Paul Newman and Joanne Woodward and competition for a hormone-rivalling Joan Collins.

The car journey was a brief but passionate encounter. Hot and heavy enough to be revived a decade later. Once encountered, it seemed, Dudley was hard to forget.

Tuesday had all the hang-ups Dudley didn't need. But he liked them. Oh, did he like them! The smile, the eyes, the body – he raved about her. And, of course, she could *understand him*.

Nonsense. But the body! New Yorker Tuesday – actually born on a Friday – spent her early years living in an apartment block following her father's death. She had an older brother and sister and, at the age of three, became the breadwinner as a child model. She had, and retains, the Bardot pout (and they share a reclusive temperament). It was a money-maker. She became a television star and had her first nervous upset when she was eight years old. She was the Drew Barrymore of her generation, a talented but troubled child star.

At nine she had an official nervous breakdown. By the age of 10 the booze had got to her, and she says she tried to kill herself when she was 12 years old with pills and drink.

This was 'Lolita' marinated in gin and other intoxicating liquids. She had 'relationships' with a galaxy of star names, from Sinatra to Albert Finney, plus perennial suntanned lover boy George Hamilton. She had co-starred with 'The King', Elvis Presley, in *Wild in the Country* in 1962. And memorably with Steve McQueen, Karl Malden, Edward G. Robinson and Ann-Margaret in *The Cincinnati Kid* in 1965. She and McQueen made quite a movie couple. As did she and Dudley.

In Hollywood she was known as the actress with the 'built-in bullshit detector'. Dudley wasn't spraying any bullshit when they reunited. And they married in Las Vegas in September 1975, having spent 18 months together. Tuesday's daughter Natasha, from her first marriage to writer Claude Harz, was then nine years old. Dudley Moore's first child was born a few months later.

Green-eyed Tuesday Weld was the Dudley Moore dream. She was incredibly alluring and very much a 'baby doll'. She has always been frank: 'I had the worst possible publicity. I decided to make up a whole life and say: "Come on, follow me." I did that to the reporters and I'd do the most outrageous things I could think of. Part of it was true, but I couldn't tell you now which was what – it was done in true rebellion against the papers because they were intruding on my privacy. Not that I wasn't outrageous, because I was. I'd just vamp. I'd do anything I could to shock and it became part of me.'

A part Dudley, deep down, rather liked. And Tuesday Weld was exceptionally sexy. And a major Hollywood star. It was an overdrive turn-on. And she was a 'serious' artist – even if she wandered into television interviews bare-footed – having appeared in the film version of John Didion's Los Angeles freeway-couch analysis *Play It As It Lays*, which in 1972 won her the Best Actress honours at the Venice Film Festival.

Dudley got the 'Californian' message for the first time when they moved to a rented house above Sunset Boulevard in Los Angeles.

Just a couple of weeks before he married Tuesday Weld, in 1975, he and Peter Cook were coming to the conclusion of their *Behind the Fridge/Good Evening* tour. He had rented a house in Hollywood Hills and, with Tuesday Weld on his arm and in his bed, was a contented fellow.

They would have dinner at Chasen's or the Rangoon Raquet Club, or lunch at the Bistro Gardens, and would sometimes 'go New York' at 'The Palm' on Santa Monica Boulevard. Mostly, they liked to eat in the garden rooms of the Bel-Air Hotel. Tuesday Weld's daughter Natasha –

'Tash' to Dudley – splashed about in their swimming pool, and stars like Cary Grant, Charlton Heston, Walter Matthau and Groucho Marx were seeking 'audiences' backstage after performances of *Good Evening*. Groucho Marx said in August 1975 of Dudley and Peter Cook: 'They are two of the funniest people working today. Two of the funniest performers I have ever seen.'

After their plaudits, Cook would drive off to his rented home and his wife, Judy Huxtable. Dudley went back to Tuesday Weld and their two-pool place. The actress, then 30, had toned down her 'Wild' image and had even convinced Dudley that yoga was good for him. Yoga! Lap-pools and Brogan Lane were still to materialise in all their Californian wonder.

Dudley *was* relaxed then and said: 'Right now I have no ambition left to do anything. I just want to laze around. That's what I've been working so hard for – to buy time to do nothing... Now, I feel I am beginning to find myself at last. It's not all easy with Tuesday. We have some pretty headlong collisions. Terrible ups and downs when we decide it's all over. But each time it seems to advance our relationship a little further.

'Tuesday's amazingly bright and honest. Totally straightforward. She's taught me that you cannot hide things. Even if you fancy someone else you must say so. You mustn't smother it.

'Her honesty sometimes makes things difficult. But now I realise it is the only way to function. For years I just couldn't be honest. I lived my life like a burglar creeping around.

'I met her years ago when I was in *Beyond the Fringe*. We had a brief romance. Then we met again in New York and we've been together ever since. We're similar in a lot of ways. We have very few friends and live in a sort of isolation. But I enjoy it. It's a happy state.

'She's almost paranoid about public life. She keeps entirely to herself. She just prefers to stay at home and wait for me. She was with me throughout the tour of *Good Evening*. Lots of places. She didn't know anyone. She'd just stay in the hotel with Tash and wait for me, but we had fun.'

Dudley's love affair with America was as strong then as his love for Tuesday Weld, and it is reflected in his remarks: 'Neither of us really knows where we want to live. She once had a place in Malibu. Now, she thinks it might be nice to live in the French countryside. My heart is where my relationship is and right at the moment it's here. Anyway, I've lived under stones for so long it's nice to be in the sun. Peter misses London: the corner newspaper shop, his mates, but I don't. Not at all. I've spent the past seven months in hotel rooms and really rather enjoyed it.

'The anonymity of living like that appeals to me. I suppose I am rather like some cheap old whore being seduced by hotel after hotel.'

It was America that seduced him and became the 'third party' in his estrangement and – in all reality – in his divorce from Peter Cook. It was sun-and-surf's-up-and-a-Californian-salad-hold-the-dressing!-days for Dudley; and liver-and-onions-another-packet-of-twenty-cigarettes-a-large-vodka-and-orange-juice-and-some-nice-gravy-and-mash for Cook. America, or rather California, was to remain Dudley's real home from then on. He liked the weather and the girls, and the girls and the weather. And in the mid-Seventies California was still a paradise. A couple of decades later it was as though some plague had been bestowed on the state – everything from earthquakes and pollution to the legal farce of the O.J. Simpson trial.

But in the Seventies it was fun. Then PSA was the airline to fly on, with the stewardesses in very politically uncorrect pink hot pants and startling blouses. Dope was smoked at 35,000 feet and throughout many sections of the city. It was an easy-going time. The era of 'sophisticated' sex, designer drugs and rock 'n' roll. Love and fun was the message.

And here was Dagenham Dud married to America's one-time sex-kitten transatlantic answer – the Stars and Stripes meow – to Bardot.

He was, for a time, like the cat that got the cream. But, like all his relationships, it was eventually to turn sour. Just as it was turning a little bitter with Peter Cook. In the Seventies they made three 'Derek (Dudley) and Clive (Cook)' records and they were delightfully – if you care for such material – obscene. It was all penis and Picasso, and cunt and cancer, and schoolboy lavatory language zipped up to an outrageous *nth* degree. 'Derek and Clive' could – and probably did – make Mary Whitehouse spend a year or more on the toilet they so happily lampooned as two lavatory attendants. It made the *Carry On* comedies that Dudley disliked seem like pleasant Merchant and Ivory moments. 'I feel it's quaint that people should be shocked by orifices and excrescences,' said Dudley with his angelic smile, adding: 'I've always been a smutty little bugger.'

The recordings, which were sold with 'no-one-under-18' warnings and stamped as *naughty*-rated, became classics for the rebel youth of the time. The record sales exceeded 50,000 copies in Britain.

America had never heard anything like it. They – well, a section of the country – loved it. It was Pete 'n' Dud's biggest hit. Totally ironic, because it could have been a taped account of their often 'colourful' conversations.

They were what they said. 'You fucking club-footed cunt!'

It may not have been 'art' but it connected with their audiences around the world.

Dudley and Tuesday, who would get an Oscar nomination for her outstanding work in *Looking for Mr Goodbar* in 1979 – the film about a disturbed woman played by Diane Keaton 'cruising' Manhattan's drinking nightspots – were, in her words, 'getting along okay'. But the separations were getting longer and more frequent.

To their friends it was clear it was not paradise. There was her Tash and their Patrick, aka 'Patch', and lots of career pressure. One friend at that time recalled: 'It wasn't bacon and eggs. Nothing was sizzling. I think there was so much going on in their lives and careers that they didn't know what to do. Dudley was a father and he wanted to be good at it, but he wasn't.

'Susan – sorry, Tuesday – was protective of the boy and that's where I think the rift began. Dudley has always concerned himself about himself, but Tuesday was concerned about Patch. That's what mattered. She had been through that as a child, and she wasn't about to put her kids through the same agonies. Dudley didn't really understand what she was going through or what she wanted to do. They were both hitting brick walls.

'The sad thing was they were different brick walls. If they had tried to break the barriers together, it might have worked.'

Dudley blamed himself for their marital problems: 'There are problems in me that are exacerbated by marriage, a whole fragile area. I am easily deflected by a lack of self-esteem. My self-esteem has always been on the droopy side, though I can usually rustle up some later in the day.'

Later, he carried on in psychiatric-couch language: 'I think resentment trickled out on all sides because I was putting myself in the arena of challenge, where the pain was very tough. I wanted to bring myself out, be myself. I resented the fact that I was denying who I was. There was a lot of anger and hostility. We didn't have a lot of calmness in our relationship, but now I realise that's not a bad thing necessarily.

'We were fighting for a purpose. Any couple that

doesn't have their spoken differences and open fights is possibly having them physically and in a more horrendous way.'

But he didn't have the benefit of hindsight when his marriage to Tuesday Weld was crumbling.

If *The Hound of the Baskervilles* had worked in 1977, perhaps Pete 'n' Dud's professional relationship would have survived. It was their fifth – and last – attempt at movie magic. Michael White, who had produced *Monty Python and the Holy Grail* and *The Rocky Horror Picture Show*, imported American director Paul Morrissey.

A graduate of the Andy Warhol school of New York underground movies, Morrissey was the man given the task of turning Pete 'n' Dud into Sherlock Holmes and Doctor Watson. He co-wrote the script with them, but it was as if they were writing in the dark. There was bickering from the start, and the only bright spot for Dudley was working with Cook and friendly faces like Terry Thomas, Spike Milligan and his university days' friend Prunella Scales.

Life did not seem too good. He was stuck in a clearly awful film and in a marriage that was going nowhere but the divorce courts.

By the end of 1978 Dudley and Tuesday were officially separated – it was the last of 20 split-ups during their time as a couple – and by the turn of the year Dudley's second wife had moved to New York with their son. The divorce became final a year later. In the settlement Tuesday waived alimony payments, received $345,700 and a trust fund was set up for their son's education. She remarried more successfully than Dudley was to.

It still clearly annoys Dudley that his former wife fell head-over-heels in love with violinist-viola-player-conductor Pinchas Zuckerman. 'She saw his bottom and that was it,' he snipes. But he admits the couple had established a solid relationship and in 1995 were providing a splendid environment for his son Patrick.

But just as Dudley felt his life was on a downturn, the Californian sun shone on him. He was actively seeking work but didn't know good fortune at first. His role in *Foul Play* – a Chevy Chase/Goldie Hawn vehicle – was as conductor Stanley Tibbets and was a cameo involving only a trio of decent scenes.

The role had been written with the comic actor Tim Conway in mind. But, just as Dudley got lucky when George Segal walked off *10*, so he had the same experience with Conway, who turned down the role. Chevy Chase, one of the *Saturday Night Live* graduates and, until *Foul Play*, a television star, suggested Dudley to director Colin Higgins.

But Dudley thought the music – and subliminally probably the sex motivations – too close to home. He finally weighed it up as his first Hollywood film and decided to go for it. Every day he blesses that move.

Tibbets' desire – and it was a passionate one – was to be the biggest swinger in San Francisco. He was sex-daft. His apartment had more kinky devices than a sex supermarket. A chance encounter in a singles bar with Goldie Hawn, who is being hunted by a killer, leads her to be asked to his home. When she gets there, Dudley presses every button but Goldie's: automatically porno films flash on a giant screen, as strobe lights bounce off ceiling mirrors and Dudley strips down to his underpants and proceeds to act like something from *Saturday Night Fever*.

'It was an easy film in some ways. I enjoyed doing it. Colin Higgins was very easy to work with. I had the feeling that he wasn't quite sure sometimes what he wanted, and maybe was a little nervous of telling you that what you did was not quite to his specifications.

'But it's very difficult sometimes to know what you can extract from a performer and how much you'll get from him if you let him have his way. It's difficult to obtain that balance. If I directed – and I'm too lazy to – really I would cast just as well as I could and then just let people do it. And make the atmosphere relaxed. Just get them to feel good whatever they did. Otherwise you're doomed. The eyes reveal everything.'

Foul Play opened Dudley's eyes to Hollywood. 'It was amazing. I'd worked for 20 years and that film suddenly brought me to the notice of people. The feedback was marvellous.' And as instant as his scenes.

It took only moments in a highly successful film to change Dudley's Hollywood profile, his 'Q' – popularity rating – and make him enough money to buy his house in Marina Del Rey. That again was coincidence. Blake Edwards lived only a few miles down the Pacific Coast Highway in Malibu. And they, of course, shared the same psychiatric sessions. And so the legend of *10* was born.

Dudley won the Hollywood Foreign Press's (HFPA's) Golden Globe in 1979 for his performance as the Bo Derek-obsessed George Webber. He was on talk shows from Johnny Carson downwards, *The Muppet Show* – everyone wanted Dudley.

He was a Hollywood sex symbol. It bemused his sister Barbara. She still lives in Upminster, only a few miles from the family home: 'Our brother-sister relationship has never changed, despite his fame. We are still very close. He has done so well in his career. He comes from a working-class family and still has the common touch.

'As his sister I'm probably a little too close to see him as a sex symbol. He's just Dudley. It could be that people easily identify with him. It could be these lovely brown eyes he has, his nice sense of humour . . . I really don't know why he's so attractive to everyone.'

Back in post-*10* Hollywood *everyone* around Dudley was desperate to cash in on his success. Of course, so was he.

Sadly, the Biblical spoof *Wholly Moses!* of 1980 was no *10*. Not even a 5 or a 6. Kindly, Gene Siskel, one of America's most influential film critics, wrote in the *Chicago Tribune* that 'The film's only redeeming feature is the comic pacing of Dudley Moore, who manages to undersell his droll sense of humour.'

Dudley was cast as a slave's son pushed adrift on the Nile in the hope that he will be adopted by the Pharaoh's daughter. The plan goes sadly wrong when he believes he is the Chosen One. Of course, Moses always gets there first.

Dudley explained how he got into such tangled rushes: 'That taught me I must rely on my instincts. And with that film my instincts told me very strongly: Don't do it. In fact, two weeks before we started I was wondering how I could get out of it. I was flattered into it. I took it because the director, Gary Weis, is a very funny man and I thought we could do something with it. As it turned out, we couldn't. I wasn't thrilled with it all.'

Dudley, who had been talked about in the same sentence as Cary Grant, in conversations about romantic leading men, had jumped back into farce.

But that was no description for where his career was heading.

CHAPTER EIGHT

Arthur and Susan and Gielgud and Liza

'VD – I'm into penicillin.'

Dudley Moore as 'Arthur', when asked by a
prostitute what he is looking for

Dudley had been comforting himself for some weeks with New Mexican farmer's daughter Susan Anton and she, in turn, with him over her broken romance with Sylvester Stallone. Dudley also wanted comforting over *Wholly Moses!*

Susan was nine inches taller than Dudley and 15 years younger, and they made an out-of-synch couple to outsiders, but from the start they were spectacularly synchronised, sexually and socially.

She had left her husband Jack Stein to spend nine months in what she calls an 'intense' romance with Stallone, who finally returned to his first wife Sasha. After nearly a year with Dudley she said of the *Rocky* and *Rambo* star: 'It's difficult to see what attracted me to him . . . I was just infatuated with Sly more than head-over-heels in love.'

Dudley, surprisingly, she found more easy-going: 'He's so wonderful to be around, a very calming influence, and he teaches you to look at yourself for the answers instead of reaching out to other people.'

The model-singer, who became an American sex

fantasy advertising Muriel cigars, visited Dudley's mother before she died. Ada Moore called her 'that tall American girl'. Susan recalled: 'It was fun seeing his baby pictures, the Oxford graduation gown and the little room he used to sleep in.'

But it was not all mothering: 'He is one of the sexiest men I have ever known. People say he is a most unlikely sex symbol, but I want to shout it out – there is nothing unlikely about Dudley's sex appeal. A man doesn't have to be tall and muscular to be sexy. Women go for men who understand their problems, feelings and emotions.

'Dudley is very sensitive about these things. He listens and cares. What's more, he is delightful to be around. We feel very free with each other and that's why we feel close together. So often people tie each other down, but somehow we are independent but dependent, and that's nice.

'He makes me laugh so much. If my hair isn't going right or my make-up doesn't look right he'll just look at me a certain way, or say something that will crack me up, and suddenly I realise it doesn't matter. He puts the whole thing in perspective. I've always been a tall woman and had to contend with that, and he's always been a small man, so he immediately understood my pain and anguish about being so tall. I'm not sure what it takes to get him angry, he's not an angry soul. His laughter comes out of the bottom of his toes – which isn't too far down for Dudley – and it's like a volcano. Sometimes I think he must have ten naked dancing girls in the other room when I hear him laughing.

'Dudley occasionally loves to be cradled, and have his hair stroked and let himself be a child again. And in turn he lets me be a little girl again, and I think that's something that every woman needs to do sometimes.'

If anyone needed a nanny or mothering it was Arthur Bach, the perpetually tipsy heir to one of America's biggest family fortunes, who wore a top hat in his bath, had a glass in his hand and a perpetual giggle on his lips and cackle in his throat. Dudley got some super co-stars for his *Arthur*. Sir John Gielgud, who had christened him Stanley Moon all those years before, played Hobson the butler, and Liza Minnelli the Cinderella that Arthur loves.

Big-name American actors, including Jack Nicholson, Al Pacino, James Caan and Richard Dreyfuss rejected the role, arguing that audiences would not be interested in an idle, irresponsible drunk waiting for his $900 million fortune to pay off. It was thumbs-down to playing a bibulous zillionaire in an over-sherried trifle of a movie.

The plot was simple enough. Arthur's family wants him to marry rich girl Susan Johnson – played by Jill Eikenberry, who went on to win great popularity in *L.A. Law* and was too precious to appear in the sequel seven years later – but he falls instead for Minelli's Linda Marolla, who helps support her family by shoplifting. Gielgud has some of the best lines. When Arthur asks Linda, from New York's blue-collar Queens district, out for a date she asks Hobson what she should wear. Hobson, always as dry as Arthur's martinis, offers this advice: 'Steal something casual.'

The movie was a huge hit – bigger than *10* – and earned more than the magic star-making box-office figure of $100 million. Once again Dudley was the spotlight boy. Big time. He took Susan Anton to the Academy Awards at the Dorothy Chandler Pavilion in 1982. He was nominated for the Best Actor Oscar, along with Warren Beatty, Burt Lancaster, Paul Newman and the dying Henry Fonda. The much-expected result was a win for Fonda for *On Golden Pond*. That other veteran, Gielgud, won Best Supporting Actor for his adored Hobson.

It had not been easy.

Steve Gordon, who had originated the *Arthur* project, lost Best Screenplay to Britain's Colin Welland for *Chariots of Fire*. More devastating was his early death a year later from a heart attack. Gordon had earlier explained his frustration at trying to 'sell' his idea to the Hollywood moguls: 'I was repeatedly told nobody would find a movie about a rich drunk sympathetic. Well, I thought the main character was sympathetic, and beyond that I argued that he was also hysterically funny, and if an audience are laughing hard enough they don't worry about whether or not a character is sympathetic.'

Steve Gordon found a convert in Mike Medavoy, one of the most astute executives in Hollywood, and an Anglophile Sunday-morning soccer-playing fanatic.

Medavoy was the head of Orion Pictures, which had backed *10*, and he believed that lightning could strike twice. And Dudley did. Even with Pauline Kael, the now retired, tough and ever-demanding film critic of *The New Yorker*.

Kael wrote: 'Considering that Arthur – a top-hatted lush who is always making whoopee – is a very thin comic construct, Moore does an amazing amount with the role. Arthur has a mad spark in his eyes and there's always something bubbling inside him; the booze just adds to this natural fizz. You don't want him to sober up, because he's such an amiable, funny drunk, chortling happily at his own nonsense.'

But this wasn't just nonsense. It was big business.

Dudley's Oscar nomination had put him in the super-league not just with the Hollywood studios but with millions of fans worldwide. Everybody, it seemed, loved *Arthur*. The one nagging doubt was over the morality of having a drunk as a leading man.

The screenplay had frightened off some heavy-hitters, but Dudley was used to controversial material. Remember Derek and Clive? He adored the screenplay and was certain he could make it work.

'I wasn't concerned about it because I thought when I read the script that I immediately saw Arthur as a happy drunk. He was a man who wasn't mean. I didn't feel he was an alcoholic, but he was in danger of being suicidal because of his drunkenness. So I didn't feel it was a threat to his health, although obviously if he did that all his life it would be.

'I didn't feel that it was something that had grave overtones. I thought the lines were so funny when he was drunk that it would be a delight to do them. I didn't prepare for the role, in the sense that I didn't go into a bar for six months and get drunk, but I have observed people around me when they are drunk, and myself on the few occasions when I have gone too far, which are very few because drink actually kills me.

'I am a very happy drunk, which is mainly at Christmas and my birthday, but I have absorbed the fumes of other people's drunkenness over the years, and so I just went to the road of least resistance and I just opened my mouth and did it. I didn't really think too much about how I would do it. I just did it and that's the way I like to perform.

'When I see a rough-cut of comedy, it is one of the most depressing things you can imagine because nothing really works – everything is a bit too long so, of course, I think that I can't bear this drunk because he's over-long, he's pushing his luck, or whatever. Then gradually things get trimmed down and you have this gestation period, where people are screaming their opinion at the director, and the poor man has to digest that and have his own opinion and make alterations to the story.

'The bias gets shifted dramatically, in some ways upsettingly, until you finally come to the final thing and it's only at the moment when it's all done – the music, the sound right and it's trimmed down – that you can actually see whether it works or not. I think that's why it is a very anxious-making situation. It is unlike a drama, where you don't have the producer's orgasmic cackle every so often. There are other things involved in comedy which are so much more fragile.'

Arthur brought Dudley worldwide recognition, but over the years and the interviews he has never put down his audiences, be they for his music or films or stage work. He wants applause. The spotlight. Centre stage.

'I never get annoyed by the fans. Never, never, never. That's why I got into it in the first place. I think the main motivation was to have people recognise me, so that I didn't have the pain of introducing myself. I was already known so it was an aid to introduction. It made it easier, simpler for me. I felt more comfortable. I was very pleased for whatever phenomenon happened with *Arthur*. That is a very attractive part of my work.

'There was no real ad-libbing in the film – it was about two or three words. The script was very strictly set. Steve Gordon was very careful about having the script set more or less word-for-word perfect, because of the fact that he felt that the economy of words and the order of words was very important to his writing, and I think he was absolutely right there.

'I think it is very wonderfully witty writing and also very heavily humorous in a very belly-laugh sort of way, so there were very few ad-libs. I remember one ad-lib, which is like one word, when I am in the restaurant with the prostitute and we clink glasses, and there is this loud clink and I say: 'Noisy', and that was about it. There's very little else that happened. The ad-lib was really in the spontaneity of the attitude more than anything, but I did feel very free.'

At the time of his great triumph as Arthur he sat down in his Marina Del Rey home and talked about his life at that moment. With hindsight, it is intriguing. He had found great fame and fortune but there were still concerns.

'I think I dealt with a lot of negativity in my youth. Right now I feel: I wonder when it's coming. I was talking about it the other day and I thought: What would happen to me if something happened to me physically? It would stop me playing the piano, for instance. I think I would sing. I am sure I would find a way of being creative in some way. I would hate to lose the joy of performing and I think I would contrive to perform, whatever happened. If I lost the use of my hands, or my face became damaged, I would still find some way of performing, because I find that the most releasing and expressive thing for me.

'I have been very lucky because 1958, when I left college, I was employed. I was very pushy, very ambitious. I took a year off, and then I wanted to work here and that was a little slow, but I still did work in England. I have never felt unemployed so I haven't had that problem and, of course, that could happen, but I don't even think about it really. I feel very fortunate.

'Accents? I very quickly made a decision that I couldn't possibly fake an American accent. I know certain people can do it to a certain degree. Sellers had no problem with it; Jane Seymour seems to do it very well; but I can't do it. I can manage Welsh (Dr Watson) and Scottish (*Beyond the Fringe*). I felt that I should use my own voice, and adjustments would have to be made in whatever I did, so I have never bothered about that.

'Of course, *10* was written for an American but then we made him an Englishman. It wasn't a difficult transition. And *Arthur* was written for a WASP – a white Anglo-Saxon Protestant – an American son of an American family but who has been brought up and educated by English tutors so he speaks with an English accent. There are so many different sorts of accents. One doesn't question Katharine Hepburn or Cary Grant.

'I can never see myself doing a musical. I can't see myself singing that stuff and flinging my arms up. I can't see that. I have been offered parts that involve music. Some years ago somebody wanted me to do Mozart. That would be a great thing to do, except I think the period costumes would look rather ridiculous. Now, if you play a part like that, then you have to consider things like costumes. On the other hand, Mozart was a wonderful buffoon and so it would be a great part in many ways, but I am not sure.

'I know I've been compared to W.C. Fields. It was said I used to do a lot of the business that Fields used to do. I couldn't do his business. He was a juggler and he did that wonderful stuff with the cane and the hat, which I couldn't begin to do, so I did that one gesture [reaching for the hat].

'I love Fields and I was sort of nervous about even doing that much, but it was a very simplified version of what he used to do. He is very much part of my comedic enjoyment. When I say that I didn't prepare for *Arthur*, I did go through the picture very carefully; I make notes about how I am going to inflect a line, so I can remember what feels right; and I might make a note there and I will rehearse it to myself, but I don't like to do it to death.

'Practically every comedian I have ever seen influences me in some way. In the early days I was very influenced by Peter Sellers in his early films; Fernandel; Marcel Marceau, who is not exactly a comedian but I was very fascinated by him; and then a whole host of other people, like Terry Thomas, Bob Hope. All of these people are so different from me. I didn't really imitate them. There was no one person I imitated. I just sort of went for my own little line.

My personality changed first before the comedy, and I have been interested in psychiatry since 1964, which is when I first went into it.

'I want to be a hero in my own life, as it were. I don't want to be John Wayne but I want to lead my own life and pull my life behind me, instead of being tugged by my life. That's really the difference. I want to play people who are less far down the psychological ladder, because I feel pretty good in myself. I don't want to play sickeningly wonderful people. In fact, in *10* and *Arthur* there is a lot of stuff that is unattractive about those people – Webber was a bore, I think, in many ways, and Arthur is irresponsible to the point where some people might find that offensive.

'I have always known professional success. I am very lucky that way, so my personal success has succeeded changes in my work, and it is such a luxury for me to play parts where I can just be myself. I can now talk to you, I can talk like this and show myself, and not feel bad about it. I could never have done that years ago. It is a comparatively recent thing – remember, I've been in therapy since 1964.

'It's rather like if you do yoga; you keep doing it all your life, because it is an exercise you need to keep up, like playing the piano. Therapy for me is a way of meeting people and wrestling with the problems of having an intimate relationship, in terms of what the other person thinks and feels. I don't mean sexually, necessarily. I just mean getting to grips with the ultimate fears in your new life and the pain in your life, and trying to see it as it is. I think that is something that I deal with on a daily basis and I don't think it gets any better.

'I went into therapy thinking that I was going to change, that I had to change, but I have obviously got to a point where I realise I can't change, and I don't have to and I don't want to, and the pain doesn't go away. You just deal with it in a different way.

'It was really a personal feeling of greyness. Rather like London weather all the time in my brain.

'The change has been that I realise I don't have to change, and the very fact that you realise that you don't have to change as a person means that things start to change a little bit. The pressures diffuse, I think. It is a very hard route. Anybody who has done it will obviously know. It has produced a great improvement in my ability to be straight with myself.

'I guess the main thing is that I know I won't go crazy, that I know what I am doing, the price I am paying for whatever I do. And there is a sort of reality to my life now that I didn't feel when I was younger. I felt sort of comatose, as if I was still half in the womb, which is probably what we all have to struggle with.'

Sir John Gielgud found the experience of working on *Arthur*, and *Arthur 2* seven years later, 'delightful'. 'I got to know Stanley Moon rather well by the end of the two films,' he said with a gentle smile. 'It was a little different for me and that made it all the more interesting. What was glorious was that everyone was so professional. Sometimes I put people off, put them ill at ease. But they were all at great pains to make things comfortable for me. I made my contribution but I think all would agree that it was Arthur's film.'

Dudley, who had suggested Gielgud, was in ecstasy about his 'discovery'. He said: 'Strangely, I first saw him in Alan Bennet's play *Forty Years On*. I had seen him do classical roles and he brought to the comedy roles exactly what he did in the classical roles. That was so funny because the delivery was the same – the same sort of intensity and poetic nostalgia.

'I don't think he thinks he's funny, he just does it and doesn't really think about getting a laugh at all. I don't think he's ever been conscious of getting a laugh. But he does know laughs arise, willy-nilly like moths, in certain situations. Without undermining his actual participation in the event, I think it really comes down to him being very relaxed about it.

'I think he is very charming in person, he's not funny in person, he's very good-natured, and good-natured people are generally very rarely funny. Most people have to go into some sort of fit of mild acerbic stuff to be sort of funny-funny. But he is a very nice man and as such his laughter is very gentle.

'He is very concerned with memories. He is enriched in his own mind and memory by these thoughts of people he has known, and he loves to talk about them. You know, you get together with any buddies from England and you'll start talking immediately about common experiences. I was at a party recently and we all started talking about World War Two experiences. God knows every English man hurtles towards that at the slightest provocation. You know how extraordinarily dangerous and exotic it was during the war. So John really is getting the same sort of fun out of calling up those memories, reminiscences about old actresses, little incidents, people who have now gone.

'I thought he'd suit the role in *Arthur* because I just felt he should not have any sentimental side to him really. It should be there without him doing anything. I didn't like the idea of someone doing it who would be maybe a little over-emotional. I felt that Hobson was a fairly contained person and that the humour would come out. After I saw him on-stage I really felt that

John was perfect. We were all discussing people and I can't remember exactly how it came up, or how he came up, or who exactly brought it up. I think a lot of people lay claim to the idea of asking him.

'I guess I lay claim to it. I remember one actor being approached and I was crossing my fingers, hoping he wouldn't be able to do it and he wasn't, and thinking we really should go for John.'

Gielgud had some jovial lines in *Arthur* and there were some raised eyebrows about such a mighty theatrical knight perfectly pronouncing gutter language. Dudley found all the fuss hysterical.

'It sort of struck me as strange. He had been very well publicised as being fond of uttering four-letter words! I mean in his modern plays that's the stuff he's done. There was one line I remember that he probably had a lot of trouble saying. I – as Arthur, I might add – was about to have a bath and he shouts out: "I suppose you want me to come in there and wash your dick for you." I don't know if he had problems with that. There were a couple of moments when he had a problem. I'm not sure the humour totally reached him, but I think the fact that he did it so genuinely was very touching.

'I think he was surprised by fan-mail, surprised and delighted. I'm certainly delighted not surprised. I think it's really great. He was really, he came into another part of his life really with that film, it's not something that one could say was a natural progression, but geographically and financially it was a new lease of life for him.

'I think John is young at heart. I do. There is something very boyish about his appearance, his attitude and his enjoyment of things. It's really very delightful. He's got a great innocence about it. It makes him very open to all sorts of incidents and memories and I think that is very endearing.

'I don't think there was anything really as funny as what happened in *Arthur* when he was on his deathbed and talking about dying in a very funny way, and as he's talking a fly starts buzzing around and lands right on the tip of his nose. It was hilarious.

'He's wonderful. He is a very sweet man. That's the first thing that springs to mind. He is such a sweet man. Whenever I talk about people I have worked with, I tend to have a good time because that's the way I like to work. He is very easy to work with, and so is Liza for that matter, because they have both been on the stage and I have too, so we can do things over and over again and not really get tired of it.

'And always there is a consistency with Gielgud and Liza. He has a host of anecdotes, of course, from his past because he has acted with a lot of people. He has got a wonderfully corny sense of humour in a way; he is not a sophisticated humorist – he is not a Woody Allen but he is a totally charming man. I love him and I would love to work with him again. It is wonderful to work with somebody where you don't even have to discuss anything. You just do it. It's great. Once you start discussing you are in real trouble.'

Dudley in trouble?

Wait six weeks. Or so.

His Hollywood fame did not distract him too much from his music. In 1981, accompanied by the Los Angeles Philharmonic Orchestra, he played a jazz medley and selections from George Gershwin at the Hollywood Bowl. In January 1982 he gave a recital of chamber music, including the work of Bach, Mozart and Delius, at the Metropolitan Museum of Art with violinist Robert Mann, cellist Joel Krosnick and clarinetist Stanley Drucker. Later that year he teamed up again with Cleo Laine for an LP of musical greats and new compositions entitled 'Smilin' Through'.

That was playing Dudley's tune. The wrong notes were to follow.

CHAPTER NINE

Super-
charged
Superstar

'If we envy your penis so much, why is it that
you spend so much time trying to get what
we've got?'

Elizabeth McGovern in *Lovesick*

You negotiate a pasta spiral of free-ways to find the heartland of Los Angeles – Downtown – and where all of them are rolled like dough into more speedway spokes stands a historic apartment building, a short way from the Biltmore Hotel. Dudley spent much time here filming scenes for *Six Weeks* – his first 'serious' role. He took it seriously, but on the set he was the one easing the tension by placing 'whoopee' cushions, or 'fart cushions' as he knew them, on the seats of the crew and co-stars. Except for that of Mary Tyler Moore, who in 1982 remained the heroine of all America, the entertainment 'queen' from *The Mary Tyler Moore Show*.

She stood in an elegant, silk dressing-gown, smoking cigarettes like some Berlin chanteuse, and explained how much she adored Dudley Moore. This was going to be *their* film. 'There are no guarantees about anything but this has the warmth and feeling of what people want to see.'

Mary Tyler Moore, whose show was one of the best television situation comedies of all time, had it all wrong.

At the time she was going through her own difficulties with diabetes and alcohol but seemed completely in control.

Out of control was Dudley, running around the crowded and cramped ninth-floor set with his giggles and 'fart' cushions. He offered a long interview about his prospects and his feelings about *Six Weeks*. But he seemed ill at ease. When anyone wondered if his career was 'peaking', the film's unit publicist almost had a heart attack. Dudley just threw the thought over his shoulders like a pinch of salt – maybe wishing for good luck.

The director of *Six Weeks* was Tony Bill, who had a solid record, including producing Robert Redford and Paul Newman's *The Sting* and the Martin Scorsese/Robert De Niro combination *Taxi Driver*, and he had co-starred with Tuesday Weld in *Soldier in the Rain* in 1963. He would become one of Dudley's closest friends and also a partner in the famous Californian restaurant '72 Market Street' in Venice, the Pacific Coast artists' colony just a wander down the road from Dudley's home.

'When we were filming I talked to Dudley about how much I enjoyed eating in places where you didn't feel you were on-stage, and how I had wanted for ten years to open a place. I already owned the property – a one-time art gallery – from my office and home. With Dudley living in the neighbourhood all we were missing was a place to have a beer and a bite after work. It went from there . . .' Dudley was a social lion. The celluloid roar was a different matter.

The movie was produced by Jon Peters, who is often dismissed as Barbra Streisand's former Svengali hairdresser boyfriend. Indeed, he was a hairdresser but one who by 21 years old was a multi-millionaire. Streisand and the movies – with partner Peter Gruber – and control for a time of Columbia Pictures arrived a little later. So did a string of Oscar-winning movies like *Rain Man*.

The package seemed perfect.

But *Six Weeks* was the first of a moving walkway of Dudley movies. He had been so popular that deals within deals had been made, and there was a run of movies to be filmed. They just weren't up to box-office speed. Maybe it was the subject matter or the timing, but the movies were not on the pulse of the spiralling Eighties. Most didn't even have a box-office pulse.

According to the blurbs *Six Weeks* was a 'bitter-sweet romantic comedy'. It had originally been scheduled as a vehicle for Nick Nolte and, later, Paul Newman, Burt Reynolds and – Hollywood coincidence again – George Segal and Sylvester Stallone, although with hindsight it is difficult to imagine 'Rambo' as sensitive politician Patrick Dalton. The plot was Fifties Hollywood: campaigning Congressman Dalton and rich cosmetics businesswoman Charlotte Dreyfuss (Mary Tyler Moore) meet. She pledges to help his political ambitions if, in turn, he takes her dying daughter Nicole (Katerine Healy) on his campaign staff.

Moore and Moore get involved. Dudley becomes a father figure to the youngster and arranges her 'dream' –

to dance at New York's Lincoln Center – before she drops dead.

Which is exactly what *Six Weeks* did.

Dudley was devastated. During filming he was so certain it was going to be a major success. You could see it in his glee as he romped around the film set. The camera crew would secretly film his antics. For Mary Tyler Moore it also appeared to be a return passport to the fabulous heights. And many critics liked the performances but, sadly for all involved, not the movie. Tony Bill still maintains that not enough access was given to the audiences.

Never say to Dudley Moore: 'I'll see you in six weeks.' It sets him off just as 'Julie Andrews' did to Stanley Moon.

But that working-class work ethic kept pushing Dudley on. The late Anthony Perkins – always remembered as Norman Bates in *Psycho* – had played *Romantic Comedy* on Broadway in 1979. It was a hit. For the movies Bernard Slade's play was adapted for Dudley and Mary Steenburgen, who had won a Best Supporting Actress Oscar for her performance in *Melvin and Howard* in 1980.

On Stage 29 at MGM studios in Culver City the story about wordsmiths – Dudley's playwright and Mary Steenburgen's writer – was filmed with Arthur Hiller at the helm. The director, who had a strong track-record including *Love Story* and *Silver Streak*, saw great potential. So did Dudley. Mary Steenburgen believed she was in another huge success. And it was fun working with

Dudley: 'I was ruining as many as fifteen takes a day. By the end of the picture I was just able to control my giggles.'

Steenburgen, who was married to British actor Malcolm McDowell and in the late 1990s became involved with Ted 'Cheers' Danson, enjoyed her time with Dudley. On film they met nude. He mistakes her for a masseuse and drops his trousers. 'The film was fun to do,' she recalled, adding: 'And Dudley made it so much of an enjoyment. Doing scene after scene – and it involved a lot of dialogue – you get to know someone, and there were never any tantrums or temper of any sort. Dudley wanted us all to be happy. I think that's his life's mission.'

But his real mission was to *find* himself.

Dudley's necessity to be wanted absorbed itself into his film career. The more he worked, the more people would like him.

And Dudley worked and worked. Whatever criticism can be made of him or his career, he was no slouch at putting in the hours. He went from *Romantic Comedy* to *Lovesick*, taking over the role that had been written for Peter 'Columbo' Falk. It had Dudley as a psychiatrist who becomes obsessed – as he was with Bo Derek in *10* – with Elizabeth McGovern, playing one of his patients. McGovern, who was 20 when the film was made in 1983, had established herself as a leading lady in Robert Redford's directorial début *Ordinary People* in 1980 and a year later as the dangerous lady in the film version of E.L. Doctorow's

Ragtime, co-starring with Dustin Hoffman and Bruce Willis.

She had all sorts of perfect pedigree and Dudley was intrigued. Although 'involved' with Susan Anton, it seems – and has never been denied by either party – that Dudley and McGovern became equally 'involved'. They were seen everywhere together. Both shrugged it off as 'movie publicity', but once again Dudley had dazzled another leading lady.

He also got to work again with a titled British thespian, Sir Alec Guinness, who had tickled Hollywood with his role in the soar-away *Star Wars* in 1980. Sir Alec was the ghost of Sigmund Freud and, like Gielgud in *Arthur*, gave an arch performance. The director and screenwriter was Marshall Brickman, the long-time Woody Allen collaborator, and the Freud ghost was like that of Bogart's in Allen's *Play It Again, Sam*, which Dudley had done on the London stage. *Déjà vu?*

Lovesick was not *Play It Again, Sam*. There were some good lines, which Dudley appreciated in his own personal view from the psychiatrist's couch. He and McGovern get into 'penis envy' and she asks him: 'If *we* envy your penis so much, why is it that *you* spend so much time trying to get what we've got?'

Dudley was in heaven with that dialogue. Of course, off-screen, he knew the answer. Elizabeth McGovern would only say: 'He is the kindest, funniest, warmest man I have ever met.'

What the movie gave Dudley was romance with psychiatry, and Elizabeth McGovern and the presence of the legendary director-writer-actor-consultant-creator-character John Huston, who was involved in the film in a cameo role and to help in the upkeep of his island home off Puerto Vallerta in Mexico. Dudley's connections with Alec Guinness were minimal, but friendly. And vice-versa.

Guinness found Dudley 'agreeable', but the public did not have the same reaction to *Lovesick*. Dudley didn't have time to worry about it. He was by then filming *Unfaithfully Yours*, a remake of the 1948 success, which had starred the impeccable Rex Harrison ('This is to introduce you to Stanley Moon . . .') and the gorgeous Linda Darnell. Big names and shoes to fill. And the role had been intended for Peter Sellers, who had died in 1980. Rex Harrison and dead man's shoes? Dudley battled on.

It has a mix-up theme, like a Brian Rix farce, with a famous conductor believing his young wife – played by Klaus Kinski's daughter and Roman Polanski's muse Nastassia – is having an affair and attempting to kill her in revenge. It wasn't that great a plot, even with Harrison and Darnell being directed by Preston Sturges in 1948. Time did not help and Dudley found himself in another dud.

He went back to the man who made him a superstar – Blake Edwards. They made *Micki and Maude* together in 1984. It involved super-sperm Dudley impregnating both 'Micki and Maude' – Amy Irving and Jane Curtin – and marrying them both, and the Rix-style roundabouts of mistaken identity, and on and on . . .

And so on to *Best Defence* which in 1984 billed Eddie Murphy as 'The Strategic Guest Star'. Dudley is an Army engineer who is developing the latest war tank. Murphy is the soldier picked to test it. But Murphy is hardly in the film, and cinema groups throughout America felt they were being cheated by the billing. 'It was quoted to me as an Eddie Murphy-Dudley Moore movie,' said Joe Arnold of the Midwestern theatre group, complaining: 'But Murphy's in it for about fifteen minutes and it's obviously a secondary story-line.'

Eddie Murphy was early Eighties 'hot', following *48 Hours* and *Trading Places* and he still had to make the first *Beverly Hills Cop*. That *Best Defence* was a dreadful film was not helped by the row over Murphy's minimal, but highly hyped, involvement.

For Dudley it didn't seem things could get worse.

They could. Courtesy of *Santa Claus: The Movie*.

There were other complications, too. While making *Six Weeks*, a stunning, statuesque, startling and sensational image – and that's using Dudley's polite words – had a small scene. Her name was Brogan Lane. 'It was love at first sight – I was mesmerised,' said Dudley. 'She was very much younger than me but my mother always said she liked having young people around because they keep you young.'

The complication was that he also had Susan Anton keeping him young. Dudley thought of *Dorian Gray* and believed two paintings in the attic might keep him even younger. He has never been one to be too concerned about how many lovers he can juggle.

But the juggling act got a break, for he filmed *Santa Claus* at Pinewood Studios, the first British location he had been on since playing Dr Watson in *The Hound of the Baskervilles* eight years earlier. The father and son team of Alexander and Ilya Salkind – the producers of the three Christopher Reeve *Superman* films – invested $50 million in *Santa*. They wanted some presents back. They got Scrooged.

The Salkinds' first move was to sign Dudley as Santa's chief elf – even before they hired David Huddleston as the ho-ho-ho man. But even Rudolph wasn't going to be able to help them. But in 1985 everything was still as bright as a Christmas tree.

Dudley was having fun. Would he be a sexy elf?

'A rampant elf? Me! A rampant elf! Certainly not. The very idea! There's no sex or dirt in this at all. I'm clean and sweet and innocent all the way through.'

He was a jolly sight in his elfin garb of brown corduroy knee-breeches, flapping jacket, silk scarf and a woolly night-cap perched on his head. Over at the biggest Santa's grotto ever dreamed of, with towering floors, rows of work benches, and 250 elves frantically wrapping up Christmas gifts for Santa's sack, it was every child's dream gone happily, nostalgically mad.

'I thought it would be fun to do a part that was sweet and innocent for a change. I'm not up to playing characters who are evil, anyway, being such a nice bloke myself. This is a very sincere fellow and straightforward too. Everyone is going to love him.'

But Dudley was no Mystic Meg.

He played a mutinous sprite who has a row with Santa. He summed it up: 'I'm a go-ahead elf up at the Pole, right? I want to modernise the old workshop, get Santa in tune with modern times. He wants to stay traditional, so off I go. And I get manipulated into helping this guy into his dastardly plot against Santa.

'I don't have much experience of elves, and it did bring me out in a cold sweat when I started. I wondered what I'd got myself into. It was a bit like being in a very small army of 250 men who are of a very similar size.

The part was specially written for him by screenwriter David Newman, which Dudley found both flattering and off-putting. 'You start thinking of a small English person, instead of what works in the character. I always feel a bit uncomfortable if people say something was written for me. This was very tricky. It could so easily have spilled over into unadulterated jollity. But it's very nice to do, because it's got childlike elements of eagerness and innocence which are lovely. It's a pure family film. There's no cruelty, sadism or cheap tricks.

'We were dealing with the stuff dreams are made of, and I hadn't found a character so difficult for a long time. I wanted to do Santa because I believe in him – and it was quite different from any role I had done before.'

Dudley believes in Santa – and in love. But by the middle of the Eighties he was on the sex scales. He and Susan Anton had all but broken up and there was the tantalising Brogan Lane to toy with. Looking back, he said: 'I'd call it a mid-life crisis. It was all because I'd passed the 50-milestone. I always planned to lie about my age – I would never be 50, I'd always be 49. It happened to me when I was 30, that was the killer for me. But not at 40, for some reason. Odd, isn't it? I was truly happy when I was about 43, I remember. Passing the 50-mark makes you feel a little more urgent about keeping your sights on what you really want to do. I picked a wonderful profession – music. You can play for ever unless you get stricken with something like arthritis. It's not like being a gymnast, or a footballer or a ballet dancer.

'Taking a piece apart, phrase by phrase, and learning it, that's what I love. It's very much like I feel about life – the desire to be more intimate with people and with life itself, even more than I have been before. Mind you, that's scarcely possible.

'I've spent a lot of time since I was 13 being either a comedian or an actor. It's now very simple for me. I just allow myself to become whatever I'm playing. I improvise a lot, make up things as I go along. My whole life has been about improvisation – as a jazz pianist, in revues, as a comedian. Peter Cook and I wrote all our material improvising on tape. Not many people know that.'

And not many people know the agony he and Susan Anton went through as they broke up. He was 50. She was 35. She wanted children. He didn't want the responsibility. But a decade later he would be a father again.

Susan Anton will not discuss her feelings about the end of her affair with Dudley. She says it is too difficult to deal with. Dudley is also unusually quiet about this matter. They had gone through much together – even a manslaughter trial. Dudley was driving Anton's 1979 Mercedes-Benz 450 SL when he was rear-ended by a 1974 Datsun 280Z, while driving towards the Pacific on the Santa Monica Freeway.

When Stephen Sanders, 22, slammed into Dudley's car at 80 m.p.h. he recalls: 'I thought I was going to die.'

But a man was killed in the accident, shortly before 1 a.m. on 19 July 1983.

'I saw the lights of that car bearing down on me from behind. I barely had time to think: My God, he's not going to slow down! I'm going to die!'

The car rammed into the back of Dudley's Mercedes. According to the police, the two cars flew off in different directions. The Datsun careered wildly to the right, rolling over twice to an embankment.

'My car jumped one entire lane and went smack into the centre divider wall. I thought that was it.' The Mercedes jerked to a halt. Miraculously, Dudley was unhurt. 'But I was shaking with fear,' he said.

'He was a very lucky man,' commented Santa Monica Battalion Fire Chief Paul Stein, adding: 'Had he not worn a seat belt he probably would have crashed through the windshield.'

But as Dudley got out of the car he recalls: 'I heard the sound I had prayed I wouldn't hear – the groans of injured people.

'Two men had been thrown about 10 feet from the Datsun – which was crushed on the roof and passenger's side. One man was terribly injured. His face was pouring blood. He was gasping for breath. I took out my handkerchief and desperately tried to stop the flow of blood.

'"Don't die on me!" I begged. I was sobbing with frustration. But there was nothing I could do. He was bleeding to death before my eyes! The man – who was the passenger – later died.'

David Reuther, 22 – driver Stephen Sanders' best friend – died from head injuries while being treated at Santa Monica Hospital Medical Center.

A tow-truck removed the Mercedes, which was badly smashed up at the back. The boot had popped up and the bumper was crushed and the front end was damaged from hitting the divider wall. Dudley said that evening: 'Thank God for my seat belt. I could have died – but I guess it's heaven's idea to keep me around a little longer.'

Of course, Dudley is a survivor in every way. He was badly shaken by the car crash but, with Susan Anton gone from his daily life, he now had the comfort of Brogan Lane. Heaven was caring for him again.

CHAPTER TEN

Brogan the Bride

'I was totally riveted, in a primary way, by her.'

Dudley Moore on Brogan Lane

Brogan – 36(D)-26-36 – and Bach – the 39 Preludes and Fugues – were what dominated Dudley's life following *Santa Claus*, which delivered no presents to anyone involved. The critics found no Christmas spirit for their reviews. Dudley applied himself to the piano and found ample comfort in Brogan's bosom.

Just over a dozen years after his first appearance he was on *This Is Your Life* again in 1986 – only one of a few stars who have been given a double helping of the sycophantic television series which is now rivalled in print by *Hello* magazine. But for Dudley it was a chance, again, to be centre-stage.

Surprisingly, he had turned down another opportunity. Frank Sinatra had asked Dudley to co-star with him in a film version of *La Cage aux Folles*. But Dudley wasn't sure: 'I was flattered when Frank called and asked me to do it. I admire Frank a great deal and naturally I considered it, but I had to say no. I had nothing against playing the part of a female impersonator, but I didn't think it would be right for me.'

Dudley felt secure enough not to be 'flattered' into the role and the project fumbled from then on. Hollywood and the movies and Dudley eluded each other for 18 months before he got himself involved in *Like Father, Like Son*. It was typical Dudley. He was engaged by the script, which had a father and his 16-year-old son switching bodies and souls. Dudley could play the kid again. His co-star was Kirk Cameron, who at the time was the teen idol of America in the television series *Growing Pains*.

Dudley was cautious. He'd seen so many hopes gurgle away: 'I feel there's a very cyclical aspect to careers. I started in 1958 and my career has gone up and down predictably over the years. I picked a project that I thought would be the most fun to deal with. It's the law of diminishing returns. You can't possibly sustain a peak all the time, but I'm not gone yet.'

He was right. *Like Father, Like Son* didn't do badly. It also didn't do *big* business.

But before the movie was completed Dudley had agreed to bring back Bach – Arthur Bach. The idea had been fermenting for some time but there were always snags.

Now, it was a reality. The title was *Arthur 2: On the Rocks*. Which Dudley was career-wise. There were no worries about money or love – Brogan was there – but he also needed something bountiful at the box office.

He was so 'up' on the idea that he became 'executive producer' of the *Arthur* sequel, which brought back Liza

Minnelli and resurrected Sir John Gielgud as Hobson's ghost.

Did he feel like a movie mogul?

'Executive producer doesn't really mean much more, in terms of the sort of extra little pieces of authority that I'd had before as an actor over script and casting, and that sort of thing. I don't like to interfere with a script too much.

'I happened to love playing Arthur. I loved playing this drunk. I don't know why. Maybe because I've known a few and they do tend to be . . . They arouse compassion in me and that's how I play Arthur, with the same compassion. When I play him I'm feeling what I feel for this man out there who's an alcoholic whom I know.' This, of course, was a thinly veiled reference to Peter Cook, whom Dudley believes turned overnight into an alcoholic while they were touring together in New Zealand in 1971. Cook, he said, started turning up drunk on-stage every evening. He went on: 'Arthur's fulfilled that mildly out-of-control thing for me, because he's somebody who is sloshed all the time – sloshed rather than in an alcoholic stupor. I think the touching quality of Arthur is that he's siphoned off from real life.

'I've been drunk, and the worst times were when I went to a dentist in the morning. I'd mixed my drinks. I love vintage port, which I never drink now because it kills me, and I'd had some vintage port. It's the oils in the port that kill you and the next morning you feel like you want to die, and both times I've been to an English dentist. No sympathy whatsoever.'

He didn't need outside help this time. He had Brogan Lane. It was another case of lust at first sight.

'When I met Brogan, it was like "Who are You? Who the hell are you? My God, what . . . what happened?" Suddenly I . . . Las Vegas it was. Her name is Brogan Lane and I met her actually on a set when I was doing *Six Weeks* and I . . . I saw her and I . . .

'I was totally, in a rather sort of primary way, I'm afraid, riveted by her.

'I could not take my eyes off her and found her extraordinarily moving to me, and I didn't meet her really till about four years later, but I had met her. I had remembered her name because I'd etched it on my forehead. I just wanted to find this girl and I tried to. I wasn't able to and then we met. She was in a restaurant with a friend and she said "Do you remember me?"'

He remembered vividly. *All* the fantasies.

'And I said: "Oh, yes. Yes, you're Brogan Lane" and we sat down and we were together from that moment on.

'I think we were both aware of the traumas that we faced. I'm boringly grave a lot of the time, and serious and intense, and passionately interested in what I'm doing to a degree that would reduce most people to their knees with vast attacks of melancholia, but I do.

'I enjoy playing with people. I enjoy verbal play. It's a way that I have of communicating. I get very frustrated. I get very depressed if I can't play with people my way. I met two English people not too long ago and I actually found myself saying: "You know, I think you're the reason why I left England."

'They were so unbelievably acerbic and abrasive and nasty and hostile, and right out there. I couldn't believe it and I thought: Oh, this is difficult to deal with. There's something massively sincere about American people, which I find very endearing but it's also sometimes slightly wearing, if you're trying to be ironic and have fun.

'I need that sort of verbal play, and I find it with certain friends and I don't with others, and I have to cope with it in whatever way. But I am very boringly serious about what I do and if you find me at a piano ever, you'll find me looking rather grim most of the time or crying, or something like that.

'It's interesting how I compare the US and the UK — in that my thoughts on it are fairly smoky. I've lived in America since 1973 and in Los Angeles specifically since 1975. I don't miss England really that much. I even dare say that now. I mean, I didn't dare to say that, because you're supposed to miss the country, but I love being in a room with a piano and my music and I don't really care too much. God! Amazing! It doesn't matter to me what the architectural environment is. I think Los Angeles is a very strange place as an environment. It's a very odd mixture. I've seen some of the worst architecture I've ever seen in my life in this place, and it can't compare with the beauties of Europe and whatnot. However, my life seems to go on in my mind, with a piano or on a film set, so I don't miss the old country that much. My relationships have sort of severed a little bit with the United Kingdom. My sister Barbara is still there and a few aunts and uncles whom I've never really spent any time with.

'Everything that I've known is sort of changing. I feel like a stranger there. I go there and I stay in a hotel now and feel like a tourist, and I do the tourist things and I had more pride taking Brogan around and saying: "Well, this is the National Gallery and this is what..." Things that I never did when I actually lived there, which is sort of pathetic, but true. I'm not a great jingoist or patriot, I'm afraid, but I love Bach.'

And the ladies. And music and opera and old friends.

The early part of 1987 was busy for Dudley. He played Ko-Ko, the Lord High Executioner, in Jonathan Miller's version of *The Mikado* in Los Angeles. It was fun, a return to his roots and a chance to show that he could perform outside the movies.

It was a major triumph.

Dudley felt he was on a roll. *Arthur 2* had been completed, and although at the time he did not know that the reception for the sequel would be less enthusiastic than for the original, he was cackling like Arthur. Life was great.

At the Little Church of the West, one of the many chapels that line the streets off The Strip in Las Vegas, he married Brogan Lane on 20 February 1988. Dudley being Dudley, he was never sure.

'He was a bit nervous when he first arrived at the chapel,' said Bonnie Brunson, the wedding chapel director. 'But he was very funny. He also had his head in the clouds, as most grooms do.'

Brogan Lane wore a white wedding gown, a flowing number, and held a bouquet of tulips and baby's breath. She had four bridesmaids in lavender gowns.

Love. Las Vegas. A strange equation. But the Rev. James Hamilton, who married the happy couple, recalled: 'They were both teary-eyed when they took their vows. Once I pronounced them man and wife Mr Moore turned to everyone and proclaimed: "This time this is the one."'

Dudley and Brogan married at noon and after a 20 minute ceremony – the first of 11 performed at the Little Church of the West that day – he was officially into his third marriage.

Guests at the wedding remember that as they wandered off from the chapel on a path of paper hearts Dudley kept trying to catch the confetti, shouting: 'This is just wonderful. This is very good stuff. This is a magic moment.'

Brogan got his drift and bashed into singing the first couple of bars of 'This Magic Moment' before tossing her bouquet into the crowd of onlookers. Dudley's agent Lou Pitt (of Independent Creative Management) was best-man and, as Dudley laughingly bent down to remove Brogan's bridal garter, he turned to Pitt and his wife Betra and giggled: 'You know what I like about this whole thing? There's nothing vulgar about it. I think I'll have this garter with some maple syrup and it will go down sweet.'

The wedding reception was at the 'intimate' Las Vegas restaurant known as 'The Olive Gardens'. The

wedding took place only days after Dudley had pro-
posed on St Valentine's Day, taking a ring with two
heart-shaped diamonds bonded together by a sapphire
from his jacket pocket and placing it on Brogan's lap.

Not long afterwards Dudley talked at great length
about his life. It was an eclectic parcel of subjects. He
introduces subjects like somersaults one rolling into
another. One moment it was his son Patrick, the next
Peter Cook and then Christmas in California – and all
those years ago in Dagenham. He has been on a professional roller-coaster all his life. He talked as though he
was on the couch . . .

CHAPTER ELEVEN

On the Couch

'I'm a little burned.'

Dudley Moore on his career

In the kitchen, and then on the roof of his long-time home in Marina Del Rey, was where Dudley wanted to talk. Some things he was sure of, while others were uncertain in his mind. One thing was definite – he enjoys living in the Californian sunshine. But as he reflected back over the years, from his own childhood to fatherhood for the second time, it was evident there had not always been clear skies.

'Living here there is no reason to miss England – the weather is great. I was glad to have a change. I was really depressed by London's weather. The countryside was extraordinary and I think one obviously misses that. I haven't been there since I was 18. I went there with my music master and a friend of mine from school. We hiked around Keswick in the Lake District, and it was very beautiful. I don't think I'll ever be ready to go back. I love it, but Rome is my favourite city, because of the architecture.

'Yeah, I don't really feel like going back. I went back to see my sister when she was 60. I was in Geneva and

I phoned her from there, saying I was in Virginia on the Eastern Seaboard and I couldn't come to see her because I was still filming, and I was very sorry and would especially like to be there at this time. I couldn't go the night before her birthday, because I might have been photographed at the airport and that would have spoiled the surprise.

'I didn't want that to happen, so I had to come over on the morning of the party. I had to drive to Zurich to get a plane to London. This was the only way I could get in before her, before she arrived at my niece's house at 11 a.m. in the morning, so I got there about ten. It was terrific. Actually, it was her first surprise party and certainly her first sixtieth. It was really nice and then I stayed on a bit.

'I'm not really career-driven right now, although in certain areas I'm still ambitious to express myself in the most accurate way that I can, accurately reflecting what I feel, and that really is happening more through my music.

'I'm finding it increasingly hard to do films. The pain of actually doing a dramatic narrative is really quite severe. Because you're enacting stories that you've probably gone through in your own life and I think maybe I've quietened down a lot. So to actually enact a narrative that is full of panic and overwhelming incident, even though it's just a comedy, almost seems "I've lived this, I don't need to do this again."

'No, I'm not frightened. I'm a little burned. But there is no rhyme or reason at all. I mean, I got sort of taken up as the new thing suddenly after *10* and *Arthur*. Those were huge hits for me, but I've never made a wrong choice. You don't know what the right choice is anyway, and I can think of other films that other people have done quite well that I was offered.

'But they weren't right for me. Maybe they would have meant some commercial success, I don't know. Commercial success is what people measure things by. I remember when I saw *10*, I was absolutely mortified, I wanted to kill myself. I thought it was terrible. You go into a theatre and you're ready to pounce on anything you do wrong, and you see one flicker of an eyelid that seems out of place, generally, and I think you come down rather heavily on yourself.

'In *Arthur*, I thought: "Who wants to see this midget drunk for an hour and a half?" I had a terrible experience, because I was sitting behind Francis Ford Coppola and at the end of it he turned around and said something fairly disparaging, and without too much enthusiasm said: "Good performance." I don't know why I was hoping that he would, but he didn't seem to laugh at it at all.

'I've been very fortunate in my career, although I have worked very hard as well. People think it's come easy, and of course you do play yourself, but that's hard. I'm not Arthur but I happen to find that character very easy to do. Things *do* go in cycles. Ten years ago I got to certain heights and you either keep going or you don't. I don't know anybody who just keeps going.

'Right now Michael Jackson is on top, or Eddie

Murphy is on top. Sylvester Stallone was No. 1 for God knows how long, and Burt Reynolds. I'm a little baffled why *10* and *Arthur* took off and others didn't. I mean, I've known other pictures that I've done, *Micki and Maude*, *Six Weeks*, and I thought: "My God, this is terrific, not getting very much reaction."

'It just depends on what people want. *Romantic Comedy* was one of the least successful – that was with Mary Steenbergen. I saw this movie *Jane* a couple of weeks ago. It was good but Mary Steenbergen was crap! It is actually rather terrific, the lines were funny, it's a very moving story, but it's not necessarily one that's going to make people run and see it.

'It's another circuit you're on. You're not on the Royal Court Theatre in Sloane Square, where you're lucky if you run four days and that's a triumph. In the commercial world, you're up against *Batman* and people have a different set of standards, which I don't think is really anything to do with it. I don't see how the Hell else I could have gone. I enjoyed doing *Lovesick*. I enjoyed *Six Weeks*, *Romantic Comedy*, *Unfaithfully Yours*, *Micki and Maude*, personally I loved *Best Defence* which read wonderfully, and so how do you make the mistake by saying "Yes" or "No"? You don't know.

'I remember when I saw *Best Defence* I was sitting with Helen Shaver. First couple of minutes were hilarious – Eddie Murphy and this wonderful bronzed Arabic girl making love, and then I'm trying to get some movement out of my wife and she said: "It's not your birthday." I said to Helen Shaver, and I was laughing very hard: "From now it's downhill." What I didn't realise was that I had said the truth, because it was. It was downhill, it didn't hold together, and I didn't know why, I don't know why. And other things I have done that people have said: "Well this, or that happened", I don't know why or how, it doesn't matter in a sense. Everybody holds up the next film as the Holy Grail. "It's gotta do it this time."

'I think I've lost a little bit, I don't know if it's enthusiasm. Anxiety perhaps? I mean, I think you just do what you do, and you just keeping on doing it. I'm much more relaxed these days. My God! I think it's age. Ken Tynan once said to me about old comedians that in the end they don't care. He said they were not as pent up or as anxious about the outcome of things as maybe a younger person is, because of having some sort of confidence in what they do.

'I don't really worry about the price of bread. I have a comfortable life. I like a good bottle of wine now and again. I don't collect things. I've driven the same car for years – it's the old Bentley from England that backfired so hard today that I collapsed with laughter coming out of the garage. It was like some World War Two plane crash – a huge bang and smoke billowing.

'Back in Britain, I got involved in an Amnesty Benefit. John Cleese was directing, and sent me a very funny letter; and I kept putting it off and I said: "I really don't know if I am going to be there" and he wrote back and said: "As it's nearer the time, we were wondering if Your Eminence would be prepared to show up at this thing, or are you the contemptible little piece of shit that the Archbishop of Canterbury says you really are?" Contemptible little piece of shit, I ask you!

'I said: "Well, I'm coming in for my sister's birthday and as long as you can keep it quiet, because I really have to have it quiet." They picked me up at the airport, it's not me being grand, because you know these buggers.

'I worked with Peter. We did, "One leg too few". It had been 1977 when we probably worked together for the last time, and it was certainly our first time on-stage in England for years. I still say that the Tarzan sketch is the funniest single sketch. It's a real classic, much like the *Monty Python* parrot sketch. It's that terrible doggedness, relentlessness. In the *Monty Python* case, the man is being absolutely patent about this horror about his disgust about what's happened. This is a late parrot, a defunct parrot, this parrot is . . . I can't remember all the phrases he uses, but it was a very funny thing.

'At the other end of the scale is the Tarzan sketch, because what Peter is saying – he wrote it when he was 18 – is the height of diplomacy rather than the height of aggression. "Yeah, I'm Tarzan with one leg and I'm auditioning" and he's saying – he has these wonderful lines – "Mr Spiggott, I couldn't help noticing when you hopped in that you are a one-legged man, and the role of Tarzan is usually offered to a person with two legs, and yet you, a unidexter, are applying for the role.

'"Mr Spiggot, when I saw you come in I said: 'Hello, what a lovely leg for the role'. I've got nothing against your right leg, Mr Spiggot, trouble is neither have you." It's this endless diplomacy, as opposed to the endless aggression which was *Monty Python*.

'Do I keep a straight face? Well, no, I don't. I mean, I find it very funny and silly and wonderful, funny, though a small footnote if I may say – or a small leg – I can only hop on my right leg because of my gammy left leg, and I can't hop on that. And I developed this water-on-the-knee on the right leg because I'd really go like a pogo stick. High as I could. When we did it, we did it for an endless number of performances and I couldn't change legs. And so my leg got very tired and in fact, when I feel it, I can feel this sort of area. And so if I'm reduced to a wheelchair it's his fault.

'It was all very happy, well not all the time. We had some very difficult times, and anybody must have that when they write their own material. We did *Not Only, But Also*, our television series, from something like 1965 or 1966, and I asked him [Peter Cook] first to be a guest on a show that I was doing. That's how it started. A friend of mine called Joe McGarth had an edit from the BBC that he could show, and he asked me to do it, and I asked Peter to do it and we did some interesting, somewhat shaky things, but it led to the *Not Only But Also* series. And he spent six months in a year writing it, including creating some sort of an opening, which was always some sort of spectacular opening involving the title 'Not Only But Also'.

'For instance, on one occasion in one of the coloured versions of the show, which didn't happen until about the third series, we opened up and it looked like we were on a roadway and Peter is on a bicycle and he's lost his way.

'He's in The Road to Mandalay Bike Race and I say: "Oh, you have to go back that way, go first right, then you see the signs . . ." and he starts cycling along this road. And you pull back and you see it's on the *Ark Royal* and there is this huge road that's been painted down the middle for the planes, and it was very funny.'

Dudley believes it was old boys' stuff. 'They probably said Peter and Dudley want to do it. How do you feel about that? We got Tower Bridge to open up, got them to suspend our bloody title, but apart from that we had a lot of stuff to do, to write. We did four series but it seems so long ago now.'

His son Patrick has not seen his early work with Cook. 'He doesn't even know about them. But I don't think he's probably too interested in what his father was doing. I talked to him yesterday and I think he's going through – God almighty, what terrible stuff he's going through. It's teenage years.

'They hate you for years to come, same way as I hated my parents. But then you realise it's all they could do.

'I just hope he finds something for himself. I'm more

anxious that he finds something for himself. I don't think he will have any interest in what I do. He came to *Crazy People*, the last film I did, and I think he enjoyed being part of the crew. He was just sort of hauling cable around, apart from driving his go-cart around.'

'We were filming on this girls' school, which was supposed to look like a mental institution, and we had these sort of little golf go-carts to take us from the wardrobe department, which was a fair way away from the set, and I let him drive around. I don't know if I should have let him, but God knows, I think he had a good time.

'I think he would like to do film music. He's very interested in music. What he doesn't realise is he has to learn to read music first and that, I think, is something he doesn't see any point of right now.

'He does play the keyboards and he is really good. His co-ordination startles me a little bit. I encouraged him, and I used to play him a lot of my music when he was younger and I can hear certain things he does and it delights me. And he's done certain things that I think are extraordinary and inventive, but he's bored with the scoring and stuff. I think every boy is. I don't know anybody who isn't.

'It's not as if he does his school work wonderfully. He doesn't seem to have any concentration, like a lot of kids. I was a good student, well I was when I first started out; I was very good before I was 11. I went to a place called Green Lane. It's Green Lane Primary School, which was on the Beacontree estate in Dagenham.

'I don't know where my study ability came from. I don't know really. My mother's family, like a lot of Victorian families, made their own entertainment. Not exactly parties, but when she was younger my mother used to play the piano a lot and her sisters used to sing. She could read; she used to have terrible music. I have her old piano book called *The Star Folio*, a purple-bound book containing all sorts of stuff: mass of shit, terrible stuff written by Victorian people like Sydney Smith, 'Bird Song at Eventide'.

'My mother encouraged me. I have a receipt for about six pounds when my dad bought the piano. I got it home . . . my sister found the receipt, and it was my father buying it from his father or something. That was the one Brogan shipped here.

'We were so poor, I could never understand why I couldn't get a bike out of my parents. They were so ashamed of the fact they couldn't afford it. But it would have quietened me down.

'But that's *yesterday*. It's like me and Peter. I think we could repeat sketches from *Not Only* . . . I think there is a lot of sentiment bound up with the performance at the time, especially since it was on tape.

'There are some things on tape that are absolutely priceless, and the things that happened between us – the way we were together – it was wonderful to see. I don't know that it got better, the more and more we worked together, because again I'm afraid the law of diminishing returns comes in.

'I became a little self-conscious about what was

needed. I was analytical about what had happened to me, naturally enough. I think I became quite boring with my analytical mind, although I was a necessary part of it in many ways, but it certainly was not anything to do necessarily with creativity. But I think there were times when that analytical side really went against us.

'I remember the times in analysis when I realised quite why I'd been funny, why I wanted to be funny, started a circus and I just didn't want to be funny any more. Didn't want to do that any more. Didn't want to perpetrate what I'd done. I was at that stage of unearthing these goodies about myself.

'I needed analysis to protect myself from the kids of my own age. That was simply it, in a sense I simply turned my back on academic things, much more to retain the urging to deflect all the bullying. You know, it's a pretty universal situation, but I think seeing that as trying to be funny to protect myself was rather annoying to me.

'When I became successful I got very po-faced at the fact that I didn't need to do it any more. I didn't know what I wanted to be. I remember a time when we had a hard time, because I was sort of at the height of success.

'It was not a good time for it to happen, but it didn't seem to matter too much, except to me personally. When we did our two-man show it seemed to work itself out.

'Peter was some support. In a sense he didn't want to

go along the same line but he felt that this was just a normal condition, and why did I have to sort of go through all these contortions to even figure this out, when to him it was self-evident. On the other hand, I felt that I was learning something doing this. When we went to New Zealand and Australia I had an extraordinary time psychologically.

'I remember specifically going through a whole lot of experiences, because it made me come into contact with the real world much more. I think it was a combination of time and my age and the country; it was all those things, I presume. I was able quite luxuriously to think about all those things, presumably because I didn't have to think about anything. I just didn't want to work any more in the same way.

'We had our differences and I just felt it was not right, and when we came back from Australia a whole year went by before we did *Not Only, But Also*. I can't remember if we did it in Australia first, or England. At the end of Australia I said: "No, I can't do it any more" and then went back to America.

'After that, I can't remember the sequence, but after America I stayed over there in '75. I ended up in Los Angeles. We were in Los Angeles for six weeks, and I was with Tuesday and she wanted to revive her interest in the film business, and this was the town to be in. I decided to stay and not go back.

'I expect Peter and I could have done something. We didn't really explore it because we went our separate ways. I always expect people to lose me, so I'm never sure why it's such a surprise when it happens.

'If somebody works with you it's great, but I fully expect them to say: "I'm off." We worked together for 20 years almost, yeah, almost 20 years, because we worked in 1958. Straight from university was *Beyond the Fringe*.'

Before his death Peter Cook made some biting comments in a glossy American magazine profile about Dudley's Californian lifestyle, and how Brogan Lane was keeping him fit on exercise and fad diets.

'That piece in *Vanity Fair* was funny. I don't really mind, because I'm used to that sort of tartness from him. I don't think Brogan is, and you know, when you're very literal and straightforward and sincere, and just plain nice from Virginia, that sort of thing, well she thought it was quite evil. I thought it was funny. It was basically an insult to her.

'I don't think he was envious, living in London. I mean, maybe the thing was I remember some headline in the paper saying: "Come Back, Dud, All Is Forgiven." I don't really feel the same feeling, as if I've betrayed the country. I remember being interviewed by someone and he was basically saying: "You're leaving the country, you're betraying it." I said: "I'm not betraying it . . . What has it got to do with anything?"

'I couldn't understand really what he was saying, except: "Here I am stuck in England, doing the same thing, why shouldn't you?"

'I think Peter probably wanted success here. He played a butler in a situation comedy, but he hated doing other people's material. I have to do that here, unless I write it all myself, but he hated it, hated it. I think he felt that it's really rather badly written stuff. He didn't like *Arthur*. He quite liked *Arthur 2*. Now, why exactly he liked my character in *Arthur 2* I can't imagine, because they were the same. But he enjoyed it. He said it depended on which side of the bed he got out off.

'I don't think any comedian has any admiration that they really want to talk about for another comedian. It's terrible. I think you can admire people if you've gone somewhere yourself, if you feel in a position of mild patronisation: "Yes, he's doing very well."

'I feel there are certain comedians over here who can't possibly be patronised because they are so good. People like Robin Williams, Whoopi Goldberg or Billy Crystal – they are all wonderful. There are so many good comedians.

'I think Peter had an enormous capacity for doing stage talking to an audience. He had an enormous desire, which I don't have. I did, but I didn't know that I did.

'I know I didn't do it in as funny a way as he did. We went in different directions certainly. I wouldn't put us in the same breath, except that we've been connected through film projects.

'He was a great extraordinary fellow and an extraordinary comedian, too. I think he got pissed off. Basically, maybe, a little pissed off at anybody who has the gumption to get up and do it. He is very, very critical. In fact, when I think of the four of us in *Beyond the Fringe* I don't know how the Hell we got together. It was bad enough dealing with ourselves, let alone with a director, Eleanor Fizan. Saying something about *Beyond the Fringe*, he used to say if I ever got married, which I have done a couple of times, marry someone as stubborn as you are, you cunt!

'People couldn't actually understand it when we used obscene language to each other, but we use it very ordinarily. You know I say to him: "You stupid fucking cunt, what are you talking about", but here they think you're saying much worse, but you're not really. You're being pally in the pathetic way that English people are . . .

'We did three recordings for Derek and Clive. It might have been the third one which was probably the least enterprising. It was really quite boring. Some of it was quite good; it depends again on what side of the bed you get out off. I mean, sometimes I absolutely fall on the floor listening to it if I'm in the mood. If I'm not, it won't really get to me.

'When I've introduced Brogan to earlier work, I don't think all of the Englishisms get to her. A lot of the stuff is very English when I look back at it, but she enjoys it. She enjoys my music a very great deal, and she's been very encouraging, wonderfully encouraging. In fact, she got me and this guy together – Kenny G.

'He had a Number One doing an instrumental, which is almost unheard-of – "Song Bird" – and he did it. He plays a soprano sax, and she wanted us to play together because she felt we had something together that would be really interesting. So I brought out a whole lot of my old tunes and I got him to come across to my place. I have a recording studio, and he came and we did a few things and it was absolutely wonderful, and we've been terrific friends since. In fact, I was in San Diego recently and his show was introduced by Sugar Ray Leonard, and I was on it, and a wonderful singer called Michael Whiteboy, who sings like a black boy. Unbelievable. He sings like Ray Charles.

'Brogan is very encouraging; in that sense I think the older stuff obviously is of some sort of historical interest. She will listen and watch and I'm amazed at her continuing interest.

'Brogan could see why I was devoted to Peter Cook. I was in many ways. I think he was an extraordinary man. She could also empathise with my irritation. When Amnesty was on, she wasn't in England, she was in Virginia seeing her folks, and then she came over after Amnesty. She'd seen Peter when he was over here. He was doing his Diet Coke commercial with Madeline Rue.

'And Peter and I had a thing, and probably anybody who is around it feels a little excluded, because we excluded everybody in a sense.

'I've seen uncertain things that I've done with him that he was amused by. He was a great one for content of things. I used to empathise with the singer, rather than the song, a lot of the time. I agreed with Peter that the material has to be great, otherwise in a sense it doesn't really matter how good you are.

'Sometimes it was difficult to write with Peter. He could get very distracted by horses; he loved horse-racing, he was always betting . . . If that was the television and that was me, he used to be like wait . . . wait . . . wait a minute . . . shit . . . and this distraction to me was endless. At one point I remember saying: "Well, I'd better go." We had had a miserable morning trying to think of something, couldn't think of any-thing at all . . . And I remember standing by the door saying: "Well, I'll see you later . . . What about, why don't we do that thing about the . . ." And we started talking . . . actually doing it . . . So I could quite often do something directly I was on my way out . . . But generally it involved me standing at the door saying: "I can't stand it."

'We recorded it on tape and then we used to listen back to it, and I used to take little headings down where we wanted to go. Peter used to look at it and say: "What about that joke about so-and-so. Why don't we put that there." And we used to then do it again and I would take headings again, so about the third time we used to have a set of headings where we knew where we were going.

'Oh, we used to fall about endlessly and sometimes, sometimes it used to be miserable. You know what it's like to try and invent something that's mildly enter-taining for people to read. Now and again, Judy, his second wife, was around, but generally it was just the two of us. I really don't know what's happened to those tapes. We tended to do this at his place normally. He generally felt more at home where he was.

'When we finished in '77 time seemed to follow the pattern of previous years, because if we spent six months, which we used to do, writing and doing the series, for the next six months I never heard from him or he never heard from me – we never communicated.

'We never used to talk to each other, never go out to dinner. It is strange in a way, suddenly there was this six months' activity . . . and then you want a break for six months. I never really ever thought anything of it. In fact, obviously now, you do a film and you get very involved with people for three months. They are life and death to you, and then they are nothing. But that's perfectly all right with me, because I'm an isolated little shit.

'After '77 I can't remember what I was doing. I think I always pick out that year because it was the year we did *Hound of the Baskervilles*.

'I spent a year doing nothing. I spent a year playing piano in the garage. Also Patrick was born around that time and I didn't really feel badly about not seeing Peter.

'I mean, I just felt we'd come to a point where we wanted a gap and we'd done that before; we'd taken a year off and we did our television series, you know. We didn't do it every year. We did it '65, '66 and then I think missed out '67 and did it '68. I can't remember. I know we did take this time off.

'He said on the phone to me once: "I'm not ashamed to have done those. I thought they were so wonderful."

'I didn't leave him, or go in a different direction, which entailed telling myself off in a sense, out of any malice. I just felt I had to do other things. He wasn't a domineering partner. He called me "Hitler". Peter was very ambitious when he was younger. It just depends when your ambition tails off. At the age of 18 he had written the Tarzan sketch, and at some ridiculously early age when he was 20 had got a revue running in London with Kenneth Williams.

'He was the only professional amongst the four of us at the age of 22. When we were in London in 1960 he formed the Establishment Club when we were doing *Beyond the Fringe*, which was a major breakthrough in revue in many ways, and then the Establishment Club was major breakthrough in cabaret evenings, and then *Private Eye* was a major breakthrough in satirical newspapers, certainly in terms of contemporary situations, so he'd done it all. He said: "I'm not as ambitious as I was." I think he was quite content, quite rightly so, playing golf a little bit here, opening this or that.

'He didn't want to do anything else and people kept saying: "Well, you could have done this or that", but he'd done an enormous amount and it was sort of unrealistic to expect him to do more.

'Peter captured our imagination in another area . . . in the things that we feel that he could have done. He was responsible for a lot of material in *Beyond the*

Fringe, much more than any of us and much more than he really admitted to. I don't know why. I don't admit to any of it.

'I'm certainly very much aware there is no way you can pre-know what people want. The only thing you can do is work on your own; and I'm having great joy just working on my own. I'm not exactly a hermit.

'I play the piano a great deal and I play a lot of Bach. I don't know what my aim is. I may have to write it down, because there seems to be no way of knowing from day to day what I want to do.

'When I was young and out of Oxford I did everything. I was living in a ten-bob flat eating cornflakes morning, noon and night, I was doing everything. I was writing music for the Royal Court Theatre, ballets and commercials. I was playing jazz, I was doing everything: making a nuisance of myself, making a fool of myself wanting to get something done, wanting to get it all out.

'I want to get it all out now, except that I'm much more relaxed about it.

'It probably comes down to the economics of it. I'm comfortable. But I can't vegetate. I can't do that. I've got to do something for the rest of my life and I feel that today is the rest of my life.

'I find it very difficult to lounge around. Today I've been reading the rest of a script, and then I was reading a book and I decided not to put the TV on. It's very easy for me to sit there and aimlessly go through the channels and find something I like.

'I have this old grandfather clock that I bought from a place here. It's an old pine one. It came over from England and it's ticking away, tick, tick . . . This old Tiffany lamp. I have three things that I love in my life. My grandfather clock, my Tiffany lamp and one painting, and if I can see all those at one time I'm happy.

'And I just tend to play the piano or read. I play the piano whenever I can. I play either lunch or dinner. Playing reminds me of the joy one can get out of playing the piano when you really feel it. I hope that my son gets that.

'He may have to do what I did, which was to go through many years of rather boring self-involvement and analysis. He is showing talent, and I just want him to really know. I may have to get really sort of stroppy with him and boring, and say: "Listen you mother-fucker, get down, sit down and . . . because I am not going to let you waste the damn talent."

'I can understand why people do that. Tuesday is a wonderful mother in many ways. I just think that to nurture that side of somebody is very difficult. If you don't really have that experience in your lifetime, I don't think you know the importance of it in some-body's life, the meaning of it. You don't know that it has to be nurtured, that it *has* to be pushed.'

Dudley pushed himself from the start, but admits: 'I only began learning the real way to practise in 1987. I don't get nervous because I've got nothing to prove, because I think what I am doing is pretty okay.'

But he says he gratefully accepts compliments, revealing: 'I remember when I met Alec Guinness on *Lovesick*, and I'd seen him in *Great Expectations* as a friend of Pip and I thought he was wonderful. He was the sort of brother I always wanted to have and never did, and he was absolutely super.

'He was very, very jolly and enthusiastic about everything and I said to Alec Guinness when we did *Lovesick* together how much I loved him in that Dickens, how much he meant to me.

'It was almost as if he didn't hear me. *He'd* heard me! But, I guess, when somebody comes up to me and says: "I loved you in this . . ." I try to listen, because I know the terrible frustration when somebody says what they really feel about what you've done. I went up to Gene Kelly once, the first time I met him, and said: "I . . . " And before I could say anything else he said: "Don't let's talk about me, let's talk about your films." So we started talking about me.

'I couldn't believe it. I was just about to go on-stage and I really wanted to say what I felt, and I felt sort of strange that he even knew me. I really wanted to say how much he'd affected me.

'There was a five-year-old kid who'd seen me in *Arthur* and knew every bloody line from it and we were trading lines . . . it was very funny.'

What Peter Cook had found hilarious about Dudley's marriage to Brogan Lane was the exercise regime. As Cook had eaten his liver and onions, chain-smoking throughout his lunch, he had stabbed away at the food and what he saw as the ridiculous punishment Dudley was impacting on his little body. Hindsight, of course, tells a different story.

'I got on my bike for half an hour today, but I mean that was unusual – an exercise bike, keeping the old heart up, I do believe in a little bit. I'm not sure I was the best influence on Brogan. She's pretty good. She used to do aerobic dancing a great deal, which I am sure is a great idea because that is a lot of energy; and I think that could make her feel better apart from anything.'

But Brogan and healthy breakfasts were not to last. Another tall lady – *Splash* star and John Kennedy Junior's long-time *amour* Daryl Hannah – co-starred with Dudley in *Crazy People*, which was directed by Dudley's friend and restaurant partner Tony Bill.

When JFK Junior turned up to take Daryl out to dinner or lunch on location in Virginia, the star of the movie would get upset. 'Dudley was sort of in a shell,' said one crew member, adding: 'When Daryl was around he was fine. When she wasn't he sulked.'

Dudley didn't remember sulking: 'I played a television advertising executive, who goes a little berserk and wants to be a bit more truthful than the firm thinks is fit. And I get sent to a sanatorium and enlist the services of all the people there to help me write a commercial. It was quite funny. It's really a story about this man and his relationship with the world, especially a girl he meets there and all the people he meets in the sanatorium.'

Dudley's met and worked with lots of crazy people.

He admits that he might be the most disturbed of all. He's sent himself in all sorts of directions.

But in conversation he returns without fail to his roots. Were they the better days? The golden days? Were things simpler before fame – and therapy – intruded?

CHAPTER TWELVE

On the Couch 2

'Dudley lives a lot in his past.'

Brogan Lane

With all the years of therapy has Dudley Moore got anything else to analyse? 'Dudley lives a lot in his past,' says Brogan Lane, continuing: 'I think that can be a very dangerous place to live. I think the only place to live is in the present. I think to know the past, try to understand the past and accept the past for what it was can help, but there are wounds that can never be healed. They remain scars. You can only adapt the information to present time and forgive it. Forget and forgive it.

'If you keep holding onto the past it keeps you stuck. It keeps you from growing and being happy. And I think that with all the therapy that Dudley had, I don't know if it helped him through being an actor and accepting himself more.

'I think the bottom line is that once you become your best friend to yourself, that is the key and to love yourself. I know it sounds so corny and all that stuff, but you become so much more whole and you have so much more to give to the world and to a relationship. I think what Dudley liked about me was just my enthusiasms, my zest, my love for life. And very seldom will you catch me in a bad mood.

'Dudley had his moments of depression and doom or whatever, and, as I said, he tends to live in his past a lot.'

And this particular afternoon in Marina Del Rey her former husband is feeling nostalgic. He is talking of Christmases past.

'I don't think I have had one with my relatives. I have a couple of uncles and aunts and cousins and so forth but we've never really had time together. We used to have family Christmases all the time until I was about 23 or 24.

'The Christmases that are most vivid to me are the early ones. It was just my mother, father, sister and me. We just used to have a little Christmas chicken – always had chicken – and our Christmas decorations were one bell, one paper bell, and paper chains going that way and this way. We always used to make these bloody things – you'd twist them and paste them – but it was sort of fun. We never had a Christmas tree and I don't know why, maybe we couldn't afford them. It would probably have filled the room up, unless we got a tiny one. We didn't have Christmas socks or anything like that. It was never turkey – always chicken. And we had this awful liqueur called "Green Goddess".

'I remember Santa Claus as St Nicholas and I don't remember Christmas trees rather than Christmas music and services, so I remember more of the evangelical side of it.

'I belonged to the local choir. It was St Thomas of Becontree, and I used to love Christmas because I loved the music. I used to play from the time I was about 15 or 16. I started playing the organ and then I used to be the assistant organist. Sometimes I used to get weddings; sometimes I'd do funerals. I remember when the organist came to me with a deal – play all the weddings and then just for half the fee. I said I'd rather play what weddings come for the whole fee, which was my first entry into commercialism.

'I was paid a guinea, one pound one shilling, which was a fortune and I remember one afternoon there were five weddings. I couldn't believe it – I had five guineas I came away with.

'I always played "Here Comes the Bloody Bride" and I always used to play Mendelssohn's "Wedding March" at the end. And in between, if we were lucky, we wouldn't play Cremmend, which was a setting of "The Lord is My Shepherd", but we might sing some sort of rather boring hymn. Weddings were not fun to play.

'I remember being in hospital as a kid and I'd heard that Santa Claus came in the night, or the night before, and left all the presents. And I waited up and saw him come through the door, and when he'd gone I went down to the end of my bed, because all the presents were at the end of the bed, and there was nothing there.

'I cried myself to sleep, I cried and cried, couldn't believe there was nothing there, and then the next morning of course it was full of toys . . .

'This was in the convalescent home. It was a wonderful time actually, in many ways, although I can only remember little moments of it. I don't know how long I was there, but probably my sister would know more than I do. I don't really know, it all sort of blurs a bit . . . I can just remember going down the corridor singing "You Are My Sunshine".

'But some Christmases at home were wonderful.

'My mother and father would try to come to the convalescent home whenever they could, which wasn't necessarily as much as one would have wanted. It probably took a long time and it probably cost a lot. I didn't understand, but the whole question of money came into this.

'Just for them to be absent for no reason at all was always difficult. People didn't talk to you about money, did they? Money was a great taboo. It was a source of great, unfortunately, great pride to them, and I remember my mother used to sort of stand outside the butcher's shop contemplating whether it was two pieces of bacon or three. And she used to balance the books, and if she was a farthing out she'd stay up and wait until she'd got it absolutely right. That was her great mission in life – to make sure she knew what was coming in and what was going out.' And that has made Dudley watchful about finances over the years.

'I think I am fairly careful. My life has changed, I suppose, since I started doing film work, but up till then I was very cautious. I got the Marina house just by the skin of my teeth.

'I could just about put the money down for it and I wasn't sure whether it was going to be affordable, but that, in those days, was $450,000 and that was about 1975.

'I remember having come over from England, I brought that Bentley, because it was the only thing that you could legitimately bring over, because it was compatible with your lifestyle, as they say. That and five thousand quid. We were restricted, so I came over with that and it seemed to be an endless thing trying to work out about the money here.

'Then things changed, when I didn't really have to think quite as hard, but my lifestyle is very much the same. I still feel guilty about having more than one watch. I mean, that feels very strange, because I remember when I got my first watch. I just went around listening to it tick all the time. And it was just a wonderful moment . . .

'It was a Christmas present and we used to put our presents on the piano, on the piano lid, the one I've got at home. They were small enough that they could be on there. It was only one present from my parents and one from my sister, and I remember this watch. I couldn't believe my luck.

'My mother and father used to smoke cigarettes and they used to make their own, because I guess it was cheaper. They used to roll their own and my mother used to have this tin full of rolled cigarettes, and I noticed that they often lighted their cigarettes from the fire.

'So I got my mother some spills, those little bits of wood, all gaily coloured, and my father tobacco, feeling this was a very male and a very female sort of offering. My mother was going through my drawers looking for some socks and she uncovered them, the spills, and I said: "Oh, those were for you . . ." and she said: "That's all right, dear, I'll have what you were giving Daddy."

'I was heartbroken, heartbroken miserable. I cannot tell you the grief over such a tiny incident, but it was enough to absolutely floor me. And I think it was because my mother didn't quite know what I'd invested in that. There was no way I could afford anything else really. I remember the time we discovered a florin [10 pence] in the front garden and dug it up. My God! The feeling about money is pretty amazing, although it wasn't really talked about and though I didn't really feel the lack of it. I eventually bought a bike for ten bob, fixed the wheel, which used to up-end me every time I forgot . . . whoop over the handlebars. And I used to buy rides on a bike with cigarette cards. I used to give this shit up the road two or three cigarette cards for a ride up and down on this bloody bike; it was Heaven, though; it was actually Heaven. I remember one morning, one Christmas morning, that it actually snowed for the first time. It was perfect. It was really perfect timing. There was something about it. I really loved those times. I've always wanted to, in some way, re-create it.

'Mistletoe . . . oh we never used to have that, because

God help us if we were caught kissing anybody under it. I had a feeling that it wasn't . . . We pretended that didn't happen – either mistletoe or kissing.

'I was never able to take a girlfriend home. I never felt I could really do that unfortunately. I never felt I could or should, it wouldn't make me feel comfortable. My mother would be so keen on making her comfortable that she'd make me so uncomfortable. I remember being away on holiday with her and I remember seeing a girl – I thought: God, she's really rather attractive. And my mother saw that I was interested and: "Hi . . . hello. This is Dudley, my son." My reaction was: Fuck me, go home, everybody go home, thank you. I think parents are over-protective and it's a decent motivation but it's very misplaced, and fortunately you don't really know about it. I don't think you really learn until much later in life when you have children of your own . . .

'I never did bring a girlfriend home, never had one in the house, never, ever. And I don't know why actually, when I come to think of it. My sister brought her boyfriends home, I remember, a couple of times, but it seemed strange – strangers in the house. We lived in very tiny rooms, and you suddenly had this foreign presence in there that you sort of felt take over. I think that sort of influenced me.

'We used to have a sofa there and a couple of chairs and that was it – your three-piece suite. It was very pleasant but I was very unsure as to who to bring home, who not to bring home. I just didn't feel right about it. I just had a feeling about it being in some way commented on by my mother, in such a way as to embarrass. I remember I had my first party there when I was 21, and it was strange because she sort of, in a strange way, invaded the party; invaded it by sitting around expectantly and sort of trying to be one of the crew. I think it was something she wasn't really used to either.

'I think having come from a family of nine kids she probably felt there was no need for parties. There were plenty of people here already and she didn't feel comfortable with it. My sister was okay about it. But I think that's a temperamental thing. If I'd been more assertive it would have been all right, but I wasn't.

His thoughts drift back to his marriage to Brogan Lane. They always kept their separate places. 'Brogan loved to potter about the house in Toluca Lake – especially when I got difficult to live with. Which I did most of the time.

'I think I come from a very strange family. I think of my mum and dad, and Christ! I'm amazed I'm in any sort of shape at all. Bless their hearts. They didn't argue. My father was the most passive man around, very tender, very sweet but very passive. You could not really understand what the Hell he was thinking. They were both very unvocal, except now and again; moments of despair, I think, when Mother would maybe let me know about something.

'But I can only remember three or four instances when she ever voiced anything.

'My father drifted through life the way, curiously

enough, I do. But he was very proud of his life. He used to go to work every day to Stratford East on the railway. He got his watch, and all that sort of stuff.

'He was an electrician and he used to electrify coaches – like put in the lighting. He used to have these very important-looking schemes that he used to come out with some evening and look at with great deliberation, and just make sure somebody was looking. And I found it very moving but aggravating too. Because I felt: Why should he have to do that? I couldn't tell him somehow, so I learned not to voice my feelings too, which is not a good idea. I've spent many years trying to undo that.

'I felt embarrassed when I kissed my dad. I used to kiss him good night and then I said: "Dad, I don't think I should kiss you any more. I'm 16. I don't feel like I should kiss you." So that was that. He was fine about it – he was fine about everything. That was an endearing part of him, he was a very endearing man.

'My mother was just the most anxious poor woman. I remember when I started to do the television series in England in 1965. And I finally bought them a TV. "I'm on TV, you've to at least watch it." Her greatest compliment was: "Oh, you were lovely on TV last night, dear, you put me right off to sleep."

'That was her biggest compliment – that I put her off to sleep. Talk about simple pleasures!

'I guess it served me well. All my generation probably learned to do something, to fend for itself.

'Without getting rather inaccurate and maudlin, I

think that it was very useful to have that time of comparative astringency. It was a useful training for me and it was useful for me that I played the piano.

'I'll never be alone because of that. It translated into feeling that things were to be created out of nothing. I was watching a programme about some Australians learning to survive in the Bush for four days – not that we had it that way – but there was something very pleasant about making your own amusements instead of being shipped off to the video arcade.

'I don't know which way it would have turned and I don't know why I had any sort of yearnings to do other things. An unfortunate comment on my background is that I've never been able to be taught. I find it very difficult to be taught. I've never been taught anything. It means my progress is sort of through experiences and through my own sort of efforts, which is to some extent useful.

'But I regret it in some ways, because it slows down one's progress to be plunged into an area of competition. I did put myself into an area where there was a lot of competition, but I think I was a little blind about it and a little unwilling to do the work.

'I think in a sense you can blur what you're hearing from the instrument with what you are imagining is coming out. You can actually stop yourself hearing it by singing along with yourself in some way, so you don't hear what you're doing.

'The piano is a technical instrument to overcome. It's a technique that has to be overcome. I've become much more microscopic in my intentions towards technique.

'I think it sad in a way that it's taken me so long to get to that point. It's taken me all this time to come out of this sort of early coma. It feels almost like a time of sleep. I think I'm sort of on hold, before pushing forward, but maybe there is no wonderful burst forward. I don't think there is.

'What is interesting when I am playing stuff that I've written maybe 20 years ago, is that it took me about a week and a half to get anywhere near the sort of take that I wanted on one particular piece, and I realised as I went over and over it that I'd got to do what I did with other music. I've got to take it little by little.

'It's actually a metaphor for life. It's saying: "What do you want to do? Go for that and be content with just that much? Or I've got that much now, I'll do the next little bit. What do you want to hear there?"

'I think the main essence is that you do homework, that you are prepared. You are on another level. I remember Horowitz talking about being prepared for a performance and I'm only quoting him because he said it – it could have been anybody else – but he said that you have to get to a point where you just do it.

'It's just there, it's just there, and you don't do it more, because you don't want to take away the thrill of actually achieving it when you perform. However, he's done the homework. It's all there. It's all under his hands. He's in control. The homework makes the mechanics of playing possible – there's less chance of error.

'I get a thrill out of what I am actually doing, and I have to be very careful not to just get a thrill out of the physicality, because I've learned some very bad habits, which is that sort of feeling of flying. I might do too much where something else would do, and then I have to say: "Hold on, do it very slowly, what do you want there? Okay, you want that." You do that instead of doing this, which takes twice the effort. It's not as effective. It looks wonderful and feels great. However, it doesn't sound what you want, so you have got to make the sacrifice.

'I think audiences are thrilling to that, to a certain extent. It is just a matter of what you want. If you watched Horowitz play, it was very little, except he is very low over the keyboards; he was a fairly unattractive sight – certainly when he spoke it was an unattractive noise. But he produced it. His way of working was very solid, very staid, and he knew, he obviously knew the secret of playing slowly.

'It's the only secret you need to know about anything really.'

Dudley is uncertain that locking himself away with his music is good for him. He admits: 'It's an obsession I can't deny myself and it's really in the service of getting it right.

'I'm like a zombie when I come out of the studio. I don't think it's a very healthy attitude or feeling that I engender in myself, or in my personal life, but I don't know how to get round it. It's sort of a blessed curse. It's something that I have to do. That I can produce great beauty, if it's right, and enormous exasperation, if it's not.

'I think either way it can tend to take me away from real life, but that's being the way I am. I don't know how I would deal with real life. I've always spent my time with the music.

'When I think of it as a kid I just wanted to. I remember going round on the back of a truck playing piano. I was just wanting to entertain, to get away from real life.

'If you listen to the stories of musicians, that's really what they want to do. And they won't speak ill of people a great deal of the time, because they can't abide the sort of exasperation that comes from it. That's why they get this sort of tunnel-vision. I do anyway.

'I have a social life, now and again, and go to the odd party, which is sort of fun, I suppose. But it's not something that massively intrigues me if I go out. It seems to me the most extraordinary thing in life is to connect with other people.

'I certainly know Brogan made efforts to pull me out of my shell. She got me skiing, but that I will never do again. I've been three times, four times, I can't remember, but I can't do it. It hurts my fucking leg. It wouldn't be so bad, but it hurts me going down the bunny slopes.

'I also went white-water rafting with Brogan – that's great fun, I must say. We did have a couple of great fun encounters. She's very much an outdoor person in that sense. She got me on a horse down a trail. I couldn't believe it. I mean, I can't even get near a horse. I remember sitting on one in 1964 or 1965. And the thing moved and I said: "Oh, hey, it's moving" and I couldn't bear it. I was so nervous about this bloody horse moving.

'I think if you realise you are not going to be able to be part of the football team, you throw energies into something else. I have.

'I've focused into a tiny area of myself and I'm satisfied now that I can't give too much time to what I would have liked to have done. I mean, it would have been nice to have been an athlete of sorts, wouldn't it?

'I'm lucky I've got my talent and I'm very well aware that some people don't have even that, but then how could you ever tell till the end of their life that they didn't have it, because who knows?' Memories beckon again.

'Maybe at the age of 85 they might suddenly spring into action. Who knows? My dad used to be up. He was gone for 14 hours of the day, walking up to the station and getting on the train, and walking back, keeping him healthy, I guess.

'But then he used to tell the events of the day to my mother, sitting on the boot-black box in the kitchen by the mangle and, once she served up dinner, that was it.

'I remember when he made a speech, quite uncharacteristically, when my sister was getting married, and I was very moved by it. I remember telling my therapist at the time and she said maybe he was frustrated, had some artistic area that was frustrated, and maybe there was this very sincere sweet side. And I was very moved by it.

'But I didn't really seem to see too much, because it was never vocalised. It was just there, and so it was economic circumstances that kept them where they were.

'My parents came to listen to me at Christmas church quite a lot, although my father went to another church in the area. In fact, when I first started getting into singing choirs, I went to his church, which was St Peter's in Becontree, same council estate. It was High Church, Roman Catholic stuff, on top of Low Church, lots of swinging of incense.

'They were both religious. My grandfather was a faith healer. He wrote books on Christian Science. I remember we used to have a lot of them in our front room that he hadn't been able to sell. He was a very strict man, very frightening in many ways.

'I think my mother rebelled against it to a certain extent, although that religious upbringing was very important and that was the reason why I went to church and why I sang in a choir. Then I started wanting to sing. I can't remember how old I was when I first joined the choir at St Thomas of Becontree, but it was something like six or seven.

'I went to my father's church but they didn't really have a choir so I was the boat-boy for a while. Carrying the incense, but I think they were worried about me, so I left there and I went to St Thomas because I dearly wanted to be in a choir. I loved the sound of voices, so I was in that choir till I was 18 and then I went to

Oxford and basically continued the same thing, playing the organ and singing in the choir.

'My parents came once or twice to watch me there, but I can't remember when, but they did come. It was the most extraordinary setting to be in, part of that college. It was the most beautiful area, Oxford, and to be in that chapel. I was playing the organ or singing. I mean, it was just magic really. But not at Christmas time because I wasn't there. The term would be over, so Christmas was always spent at my local church, St Thomas, and I used to love that. I used to love going carol singing when I was a kid. You always used to go singing. We used to be invited in for mince pies and port wine.

'It was very much a tradition with us. There was a church, it was entirely the church. My life was involved with it. Burt King, a member, a huge man I remember, very friendly, very nice, very boring – but very friendly. Boring because his friendliness was endless.

'He used to organise us kids and we used to go round and sing carols, probably knowing where we would be invited, come to think of it, and it was absolutely enchanting at times, singing out there in the snow, and singing all these wonderful carols. Burt conducting away, and then the friendly door opening, and getting invited in for a mince pie. It was absolutely gorgeous.

'I have my favourite tape, that I even play in the car here, of carols that my sister gave me. Carols sung by the Choir of Caius College, Cambridge, with an orchestra which is absolutely gorgeous. It somehow symbolises that time of happy, easy companionship. That was it, really.

'That was the whole reason for it. It was an excuse to be close to people, not that one really should have an excuse. But for me, it was: "Oh well, here's Christmas, I guess we'll have to get together."

'But that was to me a quiet time because so little happened in my house; it was very little. We never had people, never had people in. If my mother had a friend, it was on a Thursday afternoon for a cup of tea. Auntie Olive, who happened to be somebody who worked in her office or something, and that was it. She would not let anybody in the house. "I won't have anybody in my house." It was weird that they were ashamed to share their house.

'For my mother to have a couple of hours off on a Thursday afternoon was amazing, and I felt I could not intrude and, if I did, I felt I was coming in on a sacrosanct meeting.

'There was a conviviality that was there whenever we were around the table. The times that I remember most vividly were being round the table with the wireless on and listening to *The Goon Show*. It was very cosy looking out the window.'

'We never drank – not a thing. My mother drank a little drop of sherry when she went to bed in her later years. That was it. No wine, nothing. It was Lucozade or Tizer. I never drank at all. When I met Suzy Kendall we starting drinking a little bit. I mean, I got the taste for wine. I love wine. But I don't drink, really drink.

Maybe my mother's influence is there. She didn't drink at all except, as I say, a little drop of sherry. "A half drop puts me right out," she would say.

'I always remember having to be very careful if it was snowing, and not to get my feet wet. I had to wear a special boot because of my foot and it cost a lot of money. I can still see my father sitting hunched over the boot-black box in the kitchen nailing new soles on my boot. What a mix of memories . . . I'll cry in a minute.'

CHAPTER THIRTEEN

Brogan and the Blues

'You don't want to fuck your mother.'

Brogan Lane on what ended her marriage
to Dudley

Brogan Lane is standing on her front porch and the postman's eyes pop out as he spots her. She's the kind of Hollywood wife who stops traffic – 5ft 8in tall, the figure-flattering statistical combination that 'riveted' Dudley, a bouncy nine stone with red hair, sexy voice and legs up to her ears. She is a Venus de Milo dressed – today – like Just William, in man's boots and corduroy trousers, old school tie naughtily tucked into a tight tuxedo shirt, floppy felt hat with a rose stuck in it. She's cuddling a tiny dog that's gone bald – she can't put it down because it terrorises anything on two or four feet (which is presumably why it's lost its hair); she introduces the cat, which promptly beats a hasty retreat, giggles hysterically as she shows off a collection of battered old dolls that give Dudley the creeps, and launches into song in mid-sentence.

'I don't run on all cylinders – what the Hell,' she says.

Well, we didn't expect Dudley to marry anyone *ordinary*. No assembly-line product this. She's a one-off model, beautiful and a bit bizarre, a Southern gal from Virginia who sneaked in, Scarlet O'Hara-like, and swept Dudley off his feet.

'I have my hands full, if you ask me. I'm very outgoing, happy-go-lucky, bubbly, excitable, very child-like, with a "what's next?" approach to life. I *love* life, I'm a happy, happy person and I can't shut up about it.

'Dudley's just the opposite. Sometimes I get kicked under the table – calm down, leave the table, shut up – but that's what attracted him in the first place, that child-like energy, and I'm not going to change. I talk like a country bumpkin – I leave the endings off words: actin', lovin', somethin' – and it drives him crazy. It's like him playing the piano and hitting a wrong key – it grates on him.

'I told him, relax, you loved that part of me once . . . After you get over the honeymoon period – and for us it lasted about three years – you have to learn to accept each other for their values and for the people they really are, and it's difficult.

'I come from the South, he comes from Dagenham, which is kind of backwoods. We're two backwood people coming together, and if you can make that work you get an award!'

They tried very hard to make it work. The colourful Brogan gave up her career as a successful model – she'd lived and worked in Japan, Germany, Italy, Paris, London and New York – when she met Dudley and travelled with him when he was filming.

'Too many things can happen when you're apart in

this business,' she says. 'Women are a dime a dozen. They come up and act like I don't even exist. That was tough to handle at first. I feel annoyed, affronted. You can't say anything at the time – they're fans, after all – but Dudley got it from me afterwards.'

When the 'togetherness' got too much for them – and three months together, day and night, on location can sometimes be too much – they had his usual solution: his 'n' hers houses.

'I loved Dudley's company but everyone needs privacy at times,' says Brogan. 'If I had my choice, I'd have a commune where everyone has their own wing, with their own living room and bedroom, and we'd all meet up for dinner or breakfast.'

The Lane-Moore way of life obviously had its moments. The master bedrooms of both houses – one on the beach in Marina Del Rey, the other in the quiet, country-like setting of Toluca Lake, near Universal Studios – were romantic affairs with antique beds, lace quilts, perfumed candles, soft pink lights and – in the beach house – a spectacular ocean view.

There were exercise bikes in both bedrooms, so that Dudley had no excuse for shirking the exercise routine that Brogan had helped work out for him. 'Cuddly Dudley' was not the description she liked to hear of her husband. She went to the gym three times a week for a tough work-out and aerobics, and they took private yoga classes at home in Toluca Lake, played tennis regularly, indulged in mean games of table tennis at the lake house and occasionally went white-water rafting and skiing – 'though Dudley has now told me that if I ever try to take him skiing again he will personally take the ski stick and ram it up my arse.'

Both watched their diet. 'We tried to keep on the Pritikin diet – no fats or oil, lots of fruit, vegetables, fish, pasta. When we were at the beach house we had Pritikin diet food delivered by a wonderful cook and she gave me a lot of recipes to try. Dudley still loves salt and jam and heavy puddings, and he'll occasionally binge but he really tried.'

She says she resisted her impulse to 'mother and smother' Dudley. 'I protect my man, I'm very protective financially and emotionally of him. If I sense somebody being up to no good, I'm there like an attack dog. But that was another lesson I had to learn, that I can't be so involved, that it's his life. I was doing too much for him out of my need to be loved, and that's totally dangerous. I started losing my independence and it's a bore, so now I'm starting my career again – as a model, actress, singer, anything I can!'

Hers started out as a hard-luck story: she ran away from an unhappy home at 13, supported herself in odd jobs, had a baby when she was 15 ('it was scary, terrifying'). Then she was discovered by a modelling agency, travelled the world, met Dudley and found herself zipping around in a Mercedes convertible and eccentric clothes, meeting Hollywood people and real royalty, and being kicked under the table from time to time for her exuberance and her sheer delight in life. Her son

John, 21 in 1995, was at boarding school during her time with Dudley.

'I'm a survivor. I believe in always trying to do your best, work at it, give it your best shot. I've gone through life like that.'

By the time Dudley met his third wife she was a true Californian girl. Someone should have seen the impending problems.

'I love to be around people. I love them in my house. Until just recently about six or seven girls would come over and we'd lay out by the pool and have Margaritas, or some would have wine, some water; we'd do a group-therapy-type thing. We'd pass the books around and everyone has to read one chapter . . . read it out loud to everybody. And we would all find it very interesting what chapter they picked or what subject they chose. As soon as they had read it, they had to be quiet and all of us took our turn to talk about what we felt about what they had just read, and how it may apply to them or ourselves.

'We didn't have a true therapist aboard but it was good. I felt good and women, I feel, need to be more supportive of each other. I feel even more so now as the years are passing for us. And the changes in our society, as far as financial independence for women – I really feel women need to come together more and support each other, have more support groups, or not look at each other as your competition for my man.

'I truly believe you've just got to be real honest with yourself and go with your gut instinct.

'Before I met Dudley I had no problem having relationships with the outside world – female or male, never been a problem. I had as much, or more, friends as I did with Dudley.

'I had the ability to meet all sorts that maybe I didn't have a chance to meet before I met him, but I guess I look at it – people are people. I don't put them in any kind of position, any higher than myself; I didn't goo-goo gaagaa over them.

'I did move in new circles and I touched on several of them before Dudley; and of course because he'd been in the business for so long, there was much more availability of being around these people and functions, and so forth. I had met some very interesting people before, because I modelled for ten years.

'I started modelling here, and I went to Japan and stayed several months, to live in Tokyo. And then left there, came back and continued modelling here. Then I got chosen to go to Europe. They paid for everything, basically, put you under their arms to build you and create you for the market. I stayed there on and off for two and a half years, working in London and Milan, in Paris and Germany. I had a great opportunity to meet everybody and anybody.

'This was fashion and magazines, advertisements, commercials, so instead of college for me, I got my education abroad. I learned a great deal. I think it's a wonderful way of learning about life . . . real life. That's what we're living and I know you've got to work something out in the head with all of it, but it was wonderful and then I went to New York and starting working.

'I gave up my career when I met Dudley. Between you and I, I just really realised he'd prefer me not to work. He didn't tell me that, but he showed me in other ways. I felt a little lost behind him. I'd always been the centre of attention. I'd been in my own limelight. All by myself. Not in the theatrical world, but in every other aspect and for the four years that I took time off.

'You start losing it, you become dependent. And it's a bore. And I wasn't filling my time up with hobbies necessarily. Hobbies that I love – pressing flowers, doing gardening. I love to garden. I did do that but it wasn't enough, and Dudley and I were inseparable for the first three years. I mean truly, we woke up, we had breakfast, we went to lunch together, we went to business meetings together. Then I started supporting him in his career, his album.

'I wish he'd done it for himself. I wish he'd realise his talent. When you start doing that you become a mother. Who wants to fuck their mother? And men don't know the difference. You can't mother them. Who wants to have sex with you, because in the back of their heads you become a mother? I fell into it out of the need to be needed. Well, please love. Please what can I do for you? It was totally dangerous.

'I'm sorry, but as much as men say they want an independent woman, you don't see a lot of independent women with men. Bull-fuck-shit! They like independent mistresses who they can screw their eyes to.

'I'm trying singing, which Dudley thinks I have no chance in Hell. Thank you, Dudley, for your support. I see you don't want to be a father. I sang with Dudley. I mean, fuck! I did it a couple of times and he was like this . . . horrible, horrible . . . perfectionist, a triple-shit.

'I told him: "God don't make it always on the next film – find it within yourself. You've got to, because success will give you a quick high . . . quick recognition, quick feel-good, but if it doesn't come again, where are you going to be? You can deny those feelings and say okay, every dog has its day, but once that dog's had its day, that dog don't wanna lose that bone."'

Dudley was floundering. His relationship with Brogan was going nowhere. He craved 'mothering'. He chased women.

He and Brogan had taken separate custody of their pets. He had the two dogs. She had the cat. Their marriage lasted for two years, but would it have gone on so long had she known of his extra-marital activities? He had been enamoured of Daryl Hannah on the set of *Crazy People* and, of course, it was inevitable: she is a tall, stacked blonde. But there had been other, longer fancies.

The most constant was Nicole Rothschild, whom he would marry in 1994 and who would give him another son on 28 June 1995.

But before that Dudley had a good time. He was involved with 'Penthouse Pet' Sandi Korn and was linked to actress Candy Clark. Brogan and he tried a reconciliation after their final parting in 1990, but even a French maid's outfit was not enough to concentrate Dudley's mind solely on her. It was 1992 when they finally worked out a divorce settlement, in which she received $8,000 a month – half that amount if she marries again – and became the beneficiary of a $1 million life insurance policy, as well as retaining the Toluca Lake home, all its property and the family Mercedes. Dudley agreed to pay her 1991 income tax bill and for work on the North Hollywood home.

Brogan says she still loves Dudley. But in that California-speak she says she's not *in* love with him.

In 1992 he made the knockabout farce *Blame It on the Bellboy*, which had bellboy Bronson Pinchot mixing up invitations to Mr Orton (Dudley), Mr Horton (Richard Griffiths) and Mr Lawton (Bryan Brown) at the Hotel Gabrielli in Venice – Venice, Italy, that is. Even Dudley would be pressed to get a job within walking distance from his home.

The film was decorated by Patsy Kensit, but not by much else. To Dudley it seemed an excellent enterprise. There were four weeks of filming in Venice and the rest of the movie would be completed at Shepperton Studios outside London. Most of those involved were experienced film-makers, including Steve Abbott, who had produced *A Fish Called Wanda*. It's hard to blame anything on anybody, but it certainly was not the vehicle Dudley needed to jump-start his movie status.

He really was thrashing around, despite retaining a great following and financial stability. He earned around £1 million in the super-successful Tesco supermarket chain's advertising campaign, which had him chasing chickens around the aisles. Of course, there were lots of the old jokes about 'chasing birds'.

According to the former husband of Nicole Rothschild, Moore had been more cheating than chasing over the years. Charles Cleveland maintained that while he was married to Nicole and Dudley was married to Brogan Lane, the two were involved in a hectic, passionate love affair.

Towards the end of 1993 Cleveland was saying: 'I thought the little rat was a friend of ours but he's been secretly seducing Nicole for years. They have a relationship based on non-stop sex. It went on for most of our nine-year marriage and his own to Brogan Lane.'

Cleveland, 40 in 1996, insisted that Dudley 'bought' Nicole by lavishing gifts on her. 'He's been able to buy Nicole from me. He may only be 5ft 2in tall but he's a financial giant. How can I compete with him?'

Cleveland, who fathered two children with Nicole – Lauren and Christopher, who were seven and eight years old in 1995 – insisted that he tolerated the situation, explaining: 'I went along with events only because I wanted to stay close to my kids. We were in love and had a good marriage and then she met Dudley.

'I knew they saw each other as friends and that he gave her money, but our sex life was drying up and when she came home one night I asked her straight out: "Are you sleeping with Dudley?" She said: "Well, I gave him oral sex."

'I was stunned. Dudley had only married Brogan Lane a year before and here he was having sex with my wife. I got depressed and started to drink. The more I found out about their relationship, the more I drank.

'Dudley told me it took three kinds of women to make the perfect partner – one for sex, one for intellectual stimulation and one to keep the house. He said with Nicole he had all three in one – as if I wanted to hear that. His relationship with Nikki was based on sex – and his money.

'She'd call to say she was coming over to his house and he got everything ready. Twice he ran her a bath in a tub which is as big as a swimming pool and then forgot all about it. Nikki arrived to find the place flooded and Dudley running around with hundreds of towels and mops, like it's a scene from his films.

'When she was at his house they were at it for up to five days at a time. It's like a marathon, and she told me they can both lose five pounds in weight.

'Nikki taunted me by saying Dudley was a real tiger for his size and age. They got so wild once that Nikki knocked a $50,000 Tiffany lamp off the table and it smashed on the floor. Dudley just bounced up, pushed the whole mess under the bed and hopped back into bed without missing a beat. He just giggled. He loves sex.'

Cleveland said that Dudley gave Nicole monthly 'allowances', which began at $1,000 and by 1993 were around $10,000 a month. He said: 'Dudley set up an account for her at his bank in Marina Del Rey. He doesn't spend money on himself really. It's always women he has treated. He has a secret stash of $80,000 in $100 bills, which he keeps in a wooden box. He calls it his "earthquake" money. He'd give Nikki a wad out of that but always topped it back up to $80,000 right away. If there's a earthquake he doesn't want to be caught with just credit cards.

'He gave Nikki lots of presents: a Cartier watch and a key chain from Tiffany, and a car and the rest.'

Cleveland says that he and Nicole divorced in 1990 because it was 'the only option'. At the same time Dudley and Brogan Lane officially ended their marriage. The one-time Motown harmonica player said: 'Since Brogan left Dudley's life he and Nikki have been together. He always wanted to give her presents. Even better breasts.

'Her breasts were sagging after having two children and he loves big, firm breasts. He paid for her to go to a top clinic in Newport Beach and have implants. The first job wasn't a complete success so she went back for more. She went from a B-cup to a double C and said they were both really happy about it.'

Cleveland became infatuated with Nicole in 1984 when he saw her working out on 'Muscle Beach', that hedonistic stretch of sand on the Pacific between Santa Monica Pier and Venice Pier.

'She was just a teenager then but was already dating Dudley. He had waved her down from his Bentley when he saw her driving along Sunset Boulevard. They swapped phone numbers and started a romance. But we got engaged and married later that year and so Dudley was out.'

Nicole's version of events is briefer: 'I've known Dudley since 1984. We met when we were both out driving. Before we got married we were living together – sort of. I have two children from my marriage to Charles, and Dudley didn't need them running around and screaming the whole time so we had separate houses. I know people are shocked by this, but it made sense to us. When I wanted to see him I just walked up the road. It's ideal for our lives and that's what matters.'

Time has mellowed Charles Cleveland. To a degree. He has made unsubstantiated claims, which have appeared in American newspapers, that he has video tapes in which 'Dudley is seen doing drugs on the tape and having sex with women just as famous as he is.'

Cleveland has also claimed to New Zealand-based writer Stephen d'Antal that his former wife had several lesbian affairs, including one with a famous aerobics instructor. He also told d'Antal that Dudley would stand and watch or film Nicole in lesbian action with her girlfriends. He alleged to d'Antal that Dudley and Nicole were heavily into drugs, especially Ecstasy which he helped supply them. He said one batch was badly 'cut' and resulted in Nicole having a mild stroke. He told d'Antal that Dudley 'compensated' with 'lots and lots of presents'.

Cleveland made these allegations while short of money, and angry with Dudley and the situation with his ex-wife. He said he was HIV positive and had unprotected sex with Nicole shortly before her marriage to Dudley. He also claimed that Dudley had paid for at least one abortion for Nicole before the two married in 1994.

But by that year Cleveland, Dudley and Nicole seemed reconciled. Cleveland has never retracted his allegations, and Dudley and Nicole have not commented on them, other than Dudley saying: 'This is silly.'

The 'family' seemed secure, until Dudley and Nicole had their bust-up on 21 March 1994.

Dudley was angered about her Oscar-evening comments regarding the ageing Paul Newman. She was livid about his interest in a waitress at his restaurant '72 Market Street'. The police report has neighbours witnessing Dudley shouting: 'I bought you this house. Isn't it good enough? I try to make you happy.'

And Nicole screaming back: 'You don't know how to be faithful! What about that girl in Market Street? You're a drunk. Get a life!'

When the police tried to calm the couple down, Nicole shouted: 'Look what he's done to me. He's always drinking and depressed. He's done this to me before.'

The officers found scratch-marks on her neck. Dudley admitted he had been drinking. He stumbled to the floor, saying he had injured his foot. He asked not to be arrested but a policeman explained about Nicole's injuries: 'What she sustained left officers no alternative.'

But almost as suddenly as their bust-up they were reconciled – and then married. Of their run-in with the police, Nicole said in October 1995: 'It was my fault. I was drunk as a skunk.' Of the row Dudley says: 'It was all so overblown. And it was nothing more than a domestic that got out of hand. In fact, the police officer who first came to our house returned some weeks later to say how sorry he was that such a minor incident became such big news.' After the very public row they decided to have a child – by artificial insemination. 'We didn't need to do it this way, but we weren't taking any chances about Nicole getting pregnant. The truth is: Nicole didn't want to be pregnant through the hot Californian summer.'

During the pregnancy Dudley was dutiful. He spent most of the time at the home he had bought Nicole, just picking up phone messages and faxes from his own place. Each evening he serenaded the unborn baby with 'You Are My Sunshine' – the song from his memories of that Essex convalescent home all those years before. Nicole said: 'As the song got to the end we were both singing the words together.'

Despite the domestic complications it was still easier becoming a father again than becoming a star on American television. Peter Cook had found the same thing in 1981. Cook agreed to take the part of a stuck-up butler – with a nice dry sense of humour – in the situation comedy *The Two of Us*. Cook said he found

America 'ridiculous' and lasted just 20 episodes of the CBS TV 30-minute show.

In 1993 and 1994 the CBS network tried to turn Dudley into a television giant with two separate comedies. The result was not funny.

Circle of Life

'I occasionally consider returning to live in England.'

Dudley Moore in the autumn of 1995

It was in the autumn of 1992 that Dudley agreed to star in a situation comedy for America's CBS TV network. There was much flattery about it: it was to be entitled *Dudley*. This was a chance to establish himself, as his former co-star Mary Tyler Moore had, in the television hall of fame. It began production in January 1993, and he had a top-of-the-line team behind him.

The title character was a concert pianist, divorced and a father with limited experience of parenting his teenage son. Dudley insisted: 'The role was not really me.' But he admitted: 'The situation of a character not really grown up enough to take care of his son is a fairly accurate thing about myself.

'I try to be a visible parent with Patrick but I'm not very good at it. I think it's a fairly normal thing – that rift between father and son.'

Thankfully for Dudley, the premises of the television series were not taken from real life. That 'reality' he sprinted away from. The series began with his 14-year-old-son Fred, played by Harley Cross, moving in with him. His former wife Laraine, played by the wonderful Joanna Cassidy, had been raising Fred as a single mother in California and moved him to his father in New York believing he needed 'a male influence'. Of course, sitcom-land being what it is, she takes an apartment nearby and Fred takes advantage of the situation.

It was Dudley's first regular return to television work since *Not Only, But Also* and at the time he defended going back to the small screen.

'I think there's a stigma associated with television and especially situation comedies, but it hasn't affected me. I've always gone towards what I like to do. I like this particular vehicle. I like the idea of me being a pianist, because it is one of the few things I can do. I've been gradually sort of petering toward the idea of doing television here, because I'm very nervous about development deals – films take so long. On a weekly, there's a certain urgency about television. I've had a lot of film projects offered in the past but I haven't responded to any of them.' Except, sadly, to *Blame It on the Bellboy* in 1992.

It's clear from Dudley's comments at the time that he was not at all confident about the television series: 'I've been wrong about so many things in my life. You just go on and hope for it. I really think we've done the best we can. But who knows! There's always films and concerts.'

Or another sitcom. After the rapid demise of *Dudley* there came *Daddy's Girls*. It had Dudley as a man whose wife has run off with his business partner and he has the task of looking after his three daughters. He is a fashion designer and the girls are sitcom parameters: dumb-attractive-one; knockabout-bimbo-one; smart-plain-one, who becomes his partner.

Some critics rather liked it and were fond of Dudley's playing of Harvey Feinstein as a gay clothing designer and, of course, the three attractive girls. Audiences did not respond favourably. After only three episodes the series was off the air.

Dudley plunged on.

Around the same time Peter Cook made the video film *Peter Cook Talks Golf Balls* and was doing some radio shows, although his health was clearly fading.

Dudley looked rather down himself. His disillusionment with Hollywood, the movies and television helped him decide to move with Nicole and their family to Newport Beach. For him it was really leaving his long-time real-estate security blanket – one he had held onto for 22 years.

'Newport is a serene beachside village where Nikki and her mother were both born and raised. It's the first home we've shared. Our houses were 500 yards apart in the Marina. The arrival of Nicholas has completely changed our lives. I'm fairly used to having children around, because of Nikki's two. Nicholas is an amazingly good-natured baby. He doesn't have tantrums – he just lies there and squeaks. It's been terrific becoming a father again at 60. You're less anxious but somehow more in awe of the whole process.

Our new house is more rambling and palatial than my

last one. It was built to take advantage of the gorgeous view and has a pool and patio area, where you can gaze out to sea and listen to the waves crashing on the shore. I lead a very lazy and nice life here. I take absolutely no exercise, but I'm going to have to get around to something because I am beginning to stiffen up.

'I get up between 7 and 8 a.m. I've turned my natural clock around since the days when I used to play jazz all night. Now I have no difficulty getting up at 4.30 a.m. if there's a limousine waiting to take me to a film location.

'But I don't like being away from Nikki for long periods. Being close to her is the most important thing. I stayed at home as much as possible during the long wait of her pregnancy and watched a lot of television, which is about my favourite occupation. Evenings hardly exist as I get up so early. As soon as we've got the children to bed I'm ready to go myself. We have no social life and that suits me fine. I've had my social life.

'I'd be lost without Nikki. God knows how I'd cope if she was suddenly taken away from me. I really don't know how I'd bring up our son. Marriage is an institution that I seem to be drawn to. There's obviously something in me that seems to want to be married. And I do think that Nikki is much nicer than my other wives. But I'm starting to wonder if arranged marriages might be the best. You know, I actually do think that a chap has as good a chance of meeting a reasonably nice girl if the marriage is fixed than if he's out playing the field.'

Notice he didn't say the 'right' girl. Simply, a 'nice'

girl. Will there ever be a permanently correct Mrs Dudley Moore?

But for the present his passion is Nicole.

As well as Oscar the Grand Piano. Dudley played the voice of the cartoon piano in the BBC's 1995 animated series aimed at introducing youngsters to classical music. The 13-week series which screened on BBC 1 into 1996 aimed to introduce children to classical music through a story set in 21st-century Vienna. Nasty dictator Thadius Vent had outlawed music and Oscar and other 'illegal' instruments are on the run without their music. Dudley could identify with the horror of a life without music.

The classics played throughout the series. In the final episode Good and Evil face each other to music from Wagner's 'Ring Cycle'. The BBC expects it to become an annual event.

He's also returned to the big screen.

'I recently finished making a comedy film called *A Weekend in the Country* in which I play an ageing English roué, which is what I am.

'I occasionally consider returning to live in England, but after all these years in the States there's nowhere I particularly belong. My last house in England I had to sell to prove to the tax man that I wasn't a resident. However, I'm still officially "domiciled" in Britain.

'That means they expect me to come home to die.'

Postscript

By 1997 Dudley Moore was back in Britain – talking over the end of his *fourth* marriage with his *first* wife Suzy Kendall. After yet another confrontation with Nicole he was increasingly confused and concerned about the future of their relationship. Finally, it seemed clear to him and all around him that there wasn't one.

Kendall, who over all the years provided a shoulder to cry on, a hand to hold, was there for him yet again. Nicole was back in California. Following violent fights, constant rows, allegations of kinky sex and drug-taking he had tried to hold his fourth and most bizarre marriage together. Before Christmas 1996 he was still trying for laughs. He joked that he planned to take Nicole, her two children and Nicholas on a round-the-world motorcycle journey. A reconciliation rave.

But as he faced his sixty-second birthday it seemed the only trip would be to the divorce courts to separate their lives, his cash and decide on the future of

Nicholas. There was a sense of *deja vu*: he had found himself in a similar situation with Tuesday Weld and their son Patrick who – in yet another of the great ironies of Dudley Moore's life – had moved to California in 1997 to be nearer to his father. By then 'Patch' was twenty-one and trying to make his own way as an actor.

On 21 May 1996, Moore and Nicole officially separated – one week after police were called to their home after yet another squabble. His picture was taken again – as evidence. The police photographer took close-ups of his black eye and scratches on his cheeks.

It seemed once again that the marriage had become violent. The row was provoked by Dudley going into a rage over his wife's spending. He took exception not to the amount of designer clothes she was buying but the size of the credit card statements.

Finally, after months of indecision, he made up his mind that this was another marriage that was not going to work. His next move as always was to run away from it. In June 1996 he filed for divorce in Los Angeles Superior Court citing the all encompassing 'irreconcilable differences'.

At that stage he was prepared to go to court knowing that allegations about their unconventional marriage – stories of Nicole's drug-taking and sexual adventures with other women and his own involvement with prostitutes – would be revealed. By then he was so 'stressed out' he didn't care what the world thought. Then, he and Nicole began talking and there was Nicholas to consider. The stressful, difficult weeks rolled along with no decisions being made.

By the end of 1996 Dudley Moore's life was becoming increasingly complicated. Cleveland had full-blown AIDS: Nicole had insisted he remain 'part of the family'. Dudley was sympathetic to Cleveland's plight but concerned about the effect it was having on the family, including his son Nicholas.

Cleveland's condition had already affected his professional life. He had tried to put the worries out of his mind when he was cast – along with Lauren Bacall, Jeff Bridges and Pierce Brosnan in the 1997 romantic comedy *The Mirror Has Two Faces*. Perfectionist Barbra Streisand was the star and director and it was a wonderful chance for Dudley to enjoy a high profile role.

He was distracted by thoughts of Cleveland and his family and fluffed his lines during filming in New York. Streisand read the riot act and tried to carry on filming with Dudley using cue cards. It didn't help and she fired him from his $1 million role.

'I had one bad day and it cost me a part in the movie. I admit it, I forgot my lines. I wasn't on drugs or drink – I just couldn't remember them. I had other things on my mind. I certainly don't hold a grudge against her. I think I would have fired me if I were her. Getting fired is not the worst thing that could happen. I can't predict the future . . .'

The future has played strange games for there was yet another ironic haunting: George Segal who in 1979 Dudley had replaced in *10* – one of the most pivotal happenings in his life – joined the cast of *The Mirror Has Two Faces*. Replacing Dudley as Jeff Bridges' agent and drinking buddy was the now extremely affable Segal.

Instead of filming, Dudley said he had been 'working hard every day' to keep his marriage to Nicole alive. 'There are difficulties but we've already overcome an awful lot so I'm hopeful. That's the best you can be.'

But as *The Mirror Has Two Faces* was released in cinemas worldwide in 1997, hope was fading fast. Newspaper stories had appeared voicing 'concern for Dud' and his friends *were* worried about him. Once again he was in the middle of a mighty domestic mess.

He seemed lost as he wandered around London with Suzy Kendall. It had been a long journey but here he was back around the circle – just a taxi drive away from where it all began at 14, Monmouth Road, Dagenham, Essex.

In a photograph taken then he looks bemused.

And puzzled.

FILMOGRAPHY

The Wrong Box

Salamander/Columbia, Britain, 1966. Director: Bryan Forbes. Starring: Dudley Moore, Peter Cook, Ralph Richardson, Michael Caine and Peter Sellers.

30 Is a Dangerous Age, Cynthia

Walter Shenson Films/Columbia, Britain, 1967. Director: Joe McGrath. Starring: Dudley Moore, Clive Dunn, Suzy Kendall, Eddie Foy Junior, John Bird, John Wells, Duncan Macrae and Patricia Routledge.

Bedazzled

Donen Enterprises/20th Century Fox, Britain, 1967. Director: Stanley Donen. Starring: Peter Cook, Dudley Moore, Raquel Welch, Eleanor Bron and Barry Humphries.

Monte Carlo or Bust (Quei Temeraris Suille Loro Pazze, Scatenate, Scalcinated Carriole)

Dino De Laurentiis/Marianne Productions, Italy/France, 1969. Director: Ken Annakin. Starring: Tony Curtis, Dudley Moore, Peter Cook, Jack Hawkins, Gert Frobe, Eric Sykes, Hatti Jacques and Richard Wattis.

The Bed-Sitting Room

Oscar Lewenstein Productions/United Artists, Britain, 1969. Director: Richard Lester. Starring: Arthur Lowe, Spike Milligan, Dudley Moore, Roy Kinnear, Harry Secombe, Ronald Fraser, Jimmy Edwards, Michael Hordern, Mona Washbourne, Ralph Richardson and Rita Tushingham.

Alice's Adventures in Wonderland

Josef Shaftel Productions/Fox-Rank, Britain, 1972. Director: William Sterling. Starring: Michael Hordern, Michael Jayston, Fiona Fullerton, Hywell Bennett, Michael Crawford, Dudley Moore, Spike Milligan, Peter Sellers, Ralph Richardson, Dennis Waterman, Peter Bull, Flora Robson and Dennis Price.

The Hound of the Baskervilles

Michael White Limited/Helmdale, Britain, 1977. Director: Paul Morrissey. Starring: Peter Cook, Dudley Moore, Terry Thomas, Denholm Elliott, Joan

Greenwood, Spike Milligan, Prunella Scales, Penelope Keith, Hugh Griffith, Irene Handl and Kenneth Williams.

Foul Play

Shelbournes Associates/Paramount, USA, 1978. Director: Colin Higgins. Starring: Chevy Chase, Goldie Hawn, Burgess Meredith, Brian Dennehy and Dudley Moore.

10

Orion Pictures, USA, 1979. Director: Blake Edwards. Starring: Dudley Moore, Bo Derek, Julie Andrews, Robert Webber, Brian Dennehy and Sam Jones.

Wholly Moses!

Columbia, USA, 1980. Director: Gary Weis. Starring: Dudley Moore, Laraine Newman, Madeleine Khan, Dom DeLuise, John Ritter, Richard Pryor and Jack Gilford.

Arthur

Orion Pictures, USA, 1981. Director: Steve Gordon. Starring: Dudley Moore, Liza Minnelli, John Gielgud, Jill Eikenberry, Ted Ross and Stephen Elliott.

Six Weeks

Polygram/Rank, USA, 1982. Director: Tony Bill. Starring: Dudley Moore, Mary Tyler Moore and Katherine Healy.

Unfaithfully Yours
20th Century Fox, USA, 1983. Director: Howard
Zieff. Starring: Dudley Moore, Nastassia Kinski,
Albert Brooks, Armand Assante and Cassie
Yates.

Lovesick
The Ladd Company, USA, 1983. Director: Marshall
Brickman. Starring: Dudley Moore, Elizabeth
McGovern, Alec Guinness, Ron Silver, Renee Taylor
and John Huston.

Romantic Comedy
The Mirisch Corporation, USA, 1983. Director:
Arthur Hiller. Starring: Dudley Moore, Mary
Steenburgen, Ron Leibman and Robyn Douglass.

Best Defence
Paramount, USA, 1984. Director: Willard Huyck.
Starring: Dudley Moore, Kate Capshaw, Helen Shaver,
George Dzundza and Eddie Murphy.

Micki and Maude
Columbia/Delphi 111, USA, 1984. Director: Blake
Edwards. Starring: Dudley Moore, Amy Irving, Ann
Reinking and Richard Mulligan.

Santa Claus: The Movie
Santa Claus Productions/Alexander and Ilya
Salkind/Rank, Britain, 1985. Director: Jeannot Szwarc.

Starring: Dudley Moore, David Huddleston, John Lithgow, Judy Cornwell and Burgess Meredith.

Like Father, Like Son
Tri-Star, USA, 1987. Director: Rod Daniel. Starring: Dudley Moore and Kirk Cameron.

Arthur 2: On the Rocks
Halvin/Robert Shapiro/Warner Brothers, USA, 1988. Director: Bud Yorkin. Starring: Dudley Moore, Liza Minnelli, John Gielgud, Cynthia Sykes, Geraldine Fitzgerald and Stephen Elliott.

Blame It on the Bellboy
Hollywood Pictures/Silver Screen Partner 1V, USA, 1992. Director: Mark Herman. Starring: Dudley Moore, Bryan Brown, Richard Griffiths, Alison Steadman, Bronson Pinchot and Patsy Kensit.

INDEX

SHARON STONE

Douglas Thompson

Sex sells. Sharon Stone is a multi-millionairess. The two facts are intimately connected. The controversial actress is the screen's sex sensation of the nineties and a power-player in Hollywood. This is the woman who has calculated her way to the top – and her major weapon is her raunchy sex appeal. She is the epitome of the Hollywood overnight success story – one hit film and people forget the years of hard graft and bimbo bit-parts that went before. For Stone, that film was *Basic Instinct* in which she starred opposite Michael Douglas.

Sharon Stone is the fascinating story of a thoroughly nineties woman, a modern star who according to Julie Burchill has taken over from Madonna as '*the* post-feminist icon'. Written by acclaimed Hollywood-watcher Douglas Thompson, *Sharon Stone* covers all the major influences and developments in her life, including her early modelling career, her forthright views on the cult of the 'casting couch', her relationships with Warren Beatty and Jack Nicholson, and of course her many film roles.

Warner Books now offers an exciting range of quality titles by both established and new authors. All of the books in this series are available from:

Little, Brown and Company (UK),
P.O. Box 11,
Falmouth,
Cornwall TR10 9EN.
Fax No: 01326 317444
Telephone No: 01326 317200
E-mail: books@barni.avel.co.uk

Payments can be made as follows: cheque, postal order (payable to Little, Brown and Company) or by credit cards, Visa/Access. Do not send cash or currency. UK customers and B.F.P.O. please allow £1.00 for postage and packing for the first book, plus 50p for the second book, plus 30p for each additional book up to a maximum charge of £3.00 (7 books plus).

Overseas customers including Ireland, please allow £2.00 for the first book plus £1.00 for the second book, plus 50p for each additional book.

NAME (Block Letters) ....

....

ADDRESS ....

....

....

☐ I enclose my remittance for ....
☐ I wish to pay by Access/Visa Card

Number ☐☐☐☐☐☐☐☐☐☐☐☐☐☐☐☐

Card Expiry Date ☐☐☐☐